CW00801390

The Last Knight

A Tribute to Desmond FitzGerald
29th Knight of Glin

The Last Knight

A Tribute to Desmond FitzGerald
29th Knight of Glin

Robert O'Byrne

For Ceal[?]
On your birthday 27th November 2013
Robert O'Byrne

THE LILLIPUT PRESS
DUBLIN

First published 2013 by
THE LILLIPUT PRESS
62–63 Sitric Road, Arbour Hill,
Dublin 7, Ireland
www.lilliputpress.ie

A CIP record for this title is available
from The British Library.

10 9 8 7 6 5 4 3 2 1

ISBN 978 1 84351 408 4

Set in 12.5 on 17 pt Perpetua by Marsha Swan
Printed in Spain by GraphyCems

Contents

*Plate sections fall between pages 54 and 55
and pages 118 and 119*

Introduction

THE DEATH OF Desmond FitzGerald in September 2011 was widely reported both in Ireland and overseas. Yet it struck me at the time that what garnered most space in media coverage was the fact that he represented the end of a line; that with his passing disappeared an ancient Gaelic title. On the other hand, Desmond's tireless and ground-breaking work on behalf of Irish painting, architecture, the decorative arts and the built heritage received less attention in reports and obituaries. The enormous difference that his efforts in these fields had made – to the perception of and regard for Irish culture at home and abroad – did not seem to be adequately understood or celebrated.

Those of us who knew Desmond and who had the good fortune to work alongside him always recognized the significance of his endeavours. Soon after his death, Professor Roy Foster pronounced:

> Like the Kilkenny writer Hubert Butler, Desmond made and kept a passionate commitment to Ireland which was strengthened rather than weakened by his privileged family background and his sense of the multiple weave of Irish history … Ireland has lost a doughty fighter in the national interest, a supreme recorder of her aesthetic achievements and a unique, vivid and irreplaceable personality.

It may be that his personality was in some measure responsible for the relatively meagre cognisance Desmond's efforts on behalf of Ireland sometimes received, particularly within his own country. In an eloquent address delivered at his funeral, Desmond's old friend Eddie McParland observed, 'He wasn't, I'm glad to say, the easiest person in the world to please.' The comment was received with wry laughter, because many of those present had, at some point or other, experienced Desmond's displeasure. He was not a man given to mincing his words or hiding his feelings. He spoke his mind, and could speak it frankly, even on those occasions when an emollient approach would have served him better. Desmond was not a politician, and as a rule he had little time for the members of that caste.

'In my experience,' he commented in 2002, 'politicians generally don't seem to be interested in taking care of our heritage.' (There were, of course, exceptions. His friend, the current Minister for Arts, Heritage and the Gaeltacht Jimmy Deenihan, for example, rightly declared that with Desmond's death 'Ireland has lost one of its titans and greatest champions of the arts and heritage.') In 2004, Desmond wrote, 'One of the greatest problems is that we are perhaps not the most visual people in the world here in Ireland and the whole nightmare of rural housing is a prime example of this.' This is hardly the language of the populist, and Desmond could be even less temperate in speech than he was in print.

He recognized this aspect of his character and also the charge of aloofness sometimes levelled at him. 'In my life I've always known exactly which people I've wanted to be involved with and they are mostly academics,' he told a *Sunday Independent* journalist in November 2002. 'So I really couldn't care less if people want to think I'm stuck up. I get a constant stream of people asking for my help and I'm very happy to be of help, if I can. I believe firmly in education and I do a lot of lecturing. That, I believe, is one of the most inspiring elements of life: communication with people who are interested.'

Fortunately, some people were interested in the same things as Desmond and this was always a delight. 'What pleased him inordinately,' said Eddie McParland in the course of that same funeral address, 'was any genuine interest shown in the history of Irish families and their buildings, furniture, gardens, silver, plasterwork, books, music, pictures and sculpture.' Desmond readily engaged with everyone who showed interest in the subjects that had captivated him since childhood. Surely one of his most admirable traits was this preparedness to share material he had gathered, sometimes over decades, with students and academics to whom it might be of use. What mattered was that Ireland's cultural heritage receive its due validation: provided the ambition was realized, he did not care who claimed responsibility. He was a deeply unselfish man who just wanted to see results.

'FitzGerald is wondrously loyal and consistent in his loves and hates,' wrote Christopher Gibbs – a much loved friend over five decades – in an article on Glin Castle for *House & Garden* in January 1995. 'He keeps his friendships in good repair; he hates vulgarity and sameness, and those who would harm his vision of Ireland; he has a distaste for the stuffy and self-important. He is steeped in Ireland's history and its architectural pleasures, whose mysteries he has been unravelling since he was a boy.' Similarly, Desmond declared almost twenty years later, 'I have my friends and I have always been really interested in books and writing and my life here.' 'Here' was Glin, a place of abiding importance. 'Everything in his life centred on Glin and on his life here,' said Eddie McParland in his funeral address. 'It was from Glin that radiated out those passionate commitments which embraced the whole of Ireland. For this most cosmopolitan man, Ireland was the centre of the world and Glin was the centre of Ireland.'

To understand Desmond one needs to understand Glin, and so a section of what follows is devoted to the place he loved so well that his equally adored wife Olda regularly declared it her only rival. Other sections deal with Desmond's pioneering and inestimable work in different, albeit complementary, fields and explain how he became the man he was. This is not a biography, although inevitably it contains a degree of biographical information. Rather it is intended to be a celebration of Desmond's public life and a record of his achievements. Christopher Gibbs proposed to me that it should be a rallying cry, an appeal to others to pick up the baton, to follow where Desmond led. None of us can hope to match his energy, his passion, his commitment, and the sheer scope of his scholarship. But we can try to emulate at least some of his attainments. In doing so, we will best pay tribute to a truly splendid Irishman.

Early Life

ACROSS CENTURIES there has been a pattern of Knights of Glin marrying either strong and managing wives, or wives who brought satisfactory dowries to replenish depleted castle coffers. This was the case with Desmond's paternal grandfather FitzJohn Lloyd FitzGerald, 27th Knight. He inherited the Glin estate in 1895 and two years later married Lady Rachel Wyndham-Quin, daughter of the rich and adventurous 4th Earl of Dunraven who lived at neighbouring Adare Manor.

By all accounts she was charming, kind, beautiful and artistic. After her marriage she brought rare specimens of trees and shrubs collected by her father on his travels in South America and these flourish in the Glin garden today. Her skilled portraits of her family's racehorses still hang in the front hall at Glin. The tragedy was that she died at just twenty-eight within days of giving birth to the couple's only child Desmond Wyndham Otho FitzGerald (future 28th Knight).

The 27th Knight never remarried and after suffering a stroke in 1914 was confined to a wheelchair. He lived another twenty-two years, dying just ten months before the birth of his grandson. Desmond later wrote that his grandfather, a keen sportsman, had been 'a good shot and a fine fisherman'. Evidently he was also as devoted to Glin as had been generations of FitzGeralds before him.

A friend later remembered how he had 'lived in almost feudal circumstances on the not inconsiderable part of a once larger estate, the rest of which had been forfeited to the Crown through the rebellion of his ancestors of the past. Though far from rich he was generous to a fault and extraordinarily popular with all who knew him, especially his own people at Glin ...' When members of the IRA arrived to burn down the castle during the Civil War in 1923, the 27th Knight announced from his wheelchair: 'Well you will have to burn me in it, boys.' The men, checked in their resolve at the prospect of dealing with the immovable, redoubtable Knight, decided to go back to the village. There, it was said, the locals got them so drunk they were unable to return and finish their mission. Meanwhile, Desmond's father was able to use the oil and petrol they had left behind for his machinery and for his own and his father's motor cars.

Desmond's father, the 28th Knight, had a somewhat lonely childhood, raised at Glin without a mother until he was old enough to be sent to school in England. However, he had benefitted from the care and influence of his grandfather Lord Dunraven, and also of his beautiful aunt Nesta Blennerhassett of Ballyseedy, County Kerry, the 27th Knight's sister, whose portrait hangs in the hall at Glin. Ironically, Nesta would later become the 'chère-amie' of Lord Dunraven until his death, something of which her brother greatly disapproved. Desmond's father went to Lancing where one of his contemporaries was Evelyn Waugh.

After he left school, Lord Dunraven arranged for him to become a clerk at Lloyds in London, but the job was not to his liking. Passionate about motor sports (he raced at Brooklands in Surrey and was known as 'The Nippy Knight'), in 1923 he set up a car-sales business at 32 St James's Street with Captain Alistair Miller, son of a Scottish baronet, who was seven years his senior. The association ended in litigation and the loss of money that the 28th Knight could ill afford. His diaries from the time record a jolly lifestyle of endless lunching, dining out at fashionable watering holes, and going to the theatre in the company of a series of pretty showgirls.

This brief outline of their respective characters will have indicated that, aside from a passionate love for Glin, Desmond's interests were quite different from those of his father and grandfather. Although a youthful portrait at Glin shows him holding a gun, he was uninterested in sports of all kinds, and matters mechanical also remained alien to him: he never acquired even basic computer skills and puzzled over how to use a mobile telephone. He was the unlikely product of rollicking, fighting, hard-living FitzGerald ancestors and one wonders from whence came the remarkable sensitivity to art and architecture that defined his persona and left such a legacy of research and scholarly authorship. For a part explanation one must turn to his mother, whom Desmond's father met in August 1928 at Kilruddery, County Wicklow, home of his aunt Aileen, Lady Meath. Veronica Villiers was the daughter of Ernest Villiers, former Liberal MP for Brighton and grandson of the 4th Earl of Clarendon. Veronica's mother Elaine was the granddaughter of Lady Charlotte Guest, and the wealthy ironmaster and MP from Glamorganshire in Wales, John Josiah Guest. The Guests later became Lords Wimbourne. Lady Charlotte was a famous connoisseur and her collection of fans and porcelain is now in London's Victoria and Albert Museum where Desmond would later work. She was a philanthropist and a scholar of the history of Welsh literature (she translated into English the famous mediaeval saga the *Mabinogion*). Meanwhile, on her maternal side Veronica was a granddaughter of Lady Cornelia Churchill, one of the daughters of the 7th Duke of Marlborough, thereby making her a cousin of Winston Churchill, a connection of which she was rightly proud.

A powerful influence on Desmond, Veronica's story has been eloquently chronicled in Margaret Cadwaladr's 2002 book, *In Veronica's Garden*. Desmond fully co-operated with the publication of this work, which makes no attempt to play down the complexities of Veronica's character, noting how she 'clearly had a sometimes-volatile nature and an excessive self-centredness. Whether from a single event, undue discipline or neglect, her behaviour appeared to mask underlying feelings of inadequacy that she was never able to overcome.' Most of Desmond's friends who met his mother have little kind to say of her; commonly known as 'the Knight-Mère', she and her son often clashed. 'She adored rows,' says her daughter-in-law Olda, 'and if she could provoke one she was completely happy. She required constant attention and nurturing because she was very insecure, even though she put on a terrific front.'

Nevertheless, despite the irritation she caused him – often sparked by attempts to direct his life after he reached adulthood – Desmond accepted that his mother had done much good, not least by holding on to Glin when lesser women would have abandoned the struggle. And at least some of her traits were inherited by

Desmond, including an ability to persuade other people to work with and for him on his favourite schemes. The same was also true of Veronica. In February 1953, for example, when she was attempting to set up an Irish equivalent to Britain's National Trust, one of the men she asked for help, Senator Frederick Summerfield, declared, 'As you know, you can use me in any way that will be useful, and I therefore await your reply to this letter with interest.'

Exceptionally tall and good-looking, Veronica was twenty at the time of her marriage to Desmond's father in 1929. Almost from the start the relationship was volatile, a situation not helped by the couple having to share Glin Castle during their first years with the old Knight, forever reluctant to accept any change to the existing regime. But Veronica immediately responded to the allure of her husband's family home: Desmond would write that his mother 'had a good "eye" and was much struck by Glin's delicate plaster ceilings and graceful "flying" staircase'. Desmond would also remember his mother and Eva, Lady Dunraven, antique hunting in Limerick. The two women shared a love of family history, antiques, pictures and gardening, and Eva was a kindred spirit amongst the hunting-shooting-fishing Limerick neighbours.

Her husband, despite his father's objections, had previously initiated a programme of improvement to house and grounds, and this was continued after his marriage. Desmond recalled how his parents 'restored the drawing-room ceiling, removed the Sibthorpe wallpaper [hung by his great-grandmother Isabella in the late 1860s], bought the Bossi chimneypiece for the room, and made the house comfortable, entertaining and leading a lively social life both in Ireland and in England'.

Following a visit to Glin not long after the couple married, Eva, Lady Dunraven, wrote in her diary, 'Such a nice house and pretty Adam ceilings, they gave us tea in the little sitting room with charming mahogany dado and bookcase. They are making plans for doing the house up.' In 1931 she visited again and wrote, 'Went to Glin, was delighted with the lovely view along the Shannon, found Veronica and Desmond there, and they showed us around the house, and the things they had bought at Colemans sale. The place looked so nice and we admired it and its fine bits of furniture.'

Similarly, the young couple embarked on a restoration of the gardens at Glin, neglected since the death of Lady Rachel in 1901. Perhaps to escape from the baleful eye of the old Knight, they not only travelled widely within Ireland to stay with friends but also periodically took houses in Dublin and in London. Their first daughter, Fiola, was born in April 1930, followed by a second daughter, Rachel, in March 1933. By this time the marriage was under strain, Veronica frequently living apart from her husband whose diaries indicate his unhappiness with the situation. In November 1932, for example, he wrote: 'The most awful shock in my life, she no longer loves me. I feel that life is not worth living', and later that same month: 'Veronica seems to have no sense of shame or decency. I can hardly believe it ...' On another occasion he recorded in his diary, 'The only way to have a married life without divorce is to give way ...' This appears to have been what he did: although appalled by his wife's wilful and erratic behaviour he remained loyal to her and did not countenance divorce. But the pair led largely separate lives, Desmond travelling extensively around Europe and even as far as South America while Veronica was often in London where her striking beauty, high spirits and sense of fun ensured she always had plenty of admirers. (As she did until the very end of her life.)

In 1936, the old Knight died and his departure appears to have encouraged a rapprochement between Desmond and Veronica FitzGerald since less than a year later their only son, christened Desmond John Villiers, was born on 13 July 1937. One consequence of this event was that the couple remained together, a circumstance further encouraged by the outbreak of the Second World War in 1939. Desmond's father applied to join the British armed forces but was rejected on medical grounds. For some time he had been unwell with what he self-diagnosed as a lingering 'flu; only in June 1944 was his condition discovered to be bovine tuberculosis. Ill health and enforced isolation due to Ireland's neutral status during the war years, together with fuel restrictions, meant he and Veronica were obliged to spend much of the period at Glin.

As will be evident from this brief synopsis of his parents' marriage, Desmond's early years were thus spent in a strained household where resources were scarce, his father unwell and his mother restless; always interested in art during this period, she studied painting in Connemara with Charles Lamb and came to know other Irish artists such as Sean Keating and Sean O'Sullivan. Since his two sisters were older than he and away at school, Desmond had a solitary childhood, largely raised by nannies and his nursery maid Una Bourke, who would remain an important presence at Glin for decades. One beneficial consequence of this lonely boyhood was that it encouraged him to develop his interest in history, in art, in architecture, in all the subjects on which he would later write with such fluency and knowledge.

Furthermore (and as will be discussed in more depth in the later chapter 'The Conservationist'), he was fortunate to encounter a number of older individuals who stimulated those interests. Among them was former Trinity College Dublin professor John Wardell who lived not far away and on one occasion gave the young Desmond a copy of M.R. James' *Ghost Stories of an Antiquary* with the instruction, 'Don't show this to your mother.' In 2009, Desmond wrote that 'these brilliant stories haunted my life in those days and ever since have encouraged my interest in old houses, forgotten parks and gardens and antiquarian pursuits'. Another telling incident that Desmond would relate from his childhood concerned an occasion when he was travelling on the bus from Glin to Limerick and enthusiastically pointed out a ruined castle to his elderly neighbour. He always remembered the quick retort: 'Young man, that is not a castle, it is a tower house.' The elderly man was Thomas McCreevy, poet, literary and art critic, friend of Beckett and Joyce and the director of the National Gallery of Ireland. A native of neighbouring Tarbert, County Kerry, he was making his way back to the capital, and on the way giving the young Desmond one of his earliest lessons in architectural history.

Speaking to *The Irish Times'* Catherine Foley in August 2008 about his early years, Desmond recalled, 'I was quite a solitary figure … I was thrown into my own company at an early age. I was addicted to reading quite young.' From these words one receives the impression of a small boy escaping from the palpable unhappiness of his parents' marriage and his father's ill health. 'He had a lonely childhood,' says his widow Olda, 'and I know he read and read.' During the war years he was usually taken for a summer holiday by his mother to Ballybunion, County Kerry, where, he remembered in the same *Irish Times* interview, they would stay in the old Castle Hotel. When Veronica discovered that the German chargé d'affaires was among the guests, she informed the manager 'that she would not have dinner in the company of a German, so she ordered her dinner in her bedroom. All the other people in the hotel followed her example, which caused quite a ripple.'

Even before the conclusion of the war, Desmond started to see still less of his father since the latter travelled abroad – to the dry air of Arizona, to a sanatorium in Switzerland – in what ultimately proved a futile effort to cure his tuberculosis. 'I only knew him when I got bad reports from school,' Desmond told Victoria Mary Clarke of the *Sunday Independent* in September 2002. On the other hand, given the frequency of those bad reports, he must have had regular encounters with his father. By this stage, it was time for Desmond to follow the example of his predecessors and be sent away to boarding school. For some reason he seems to have attended a succession of preparatory schools and later remembered being unhappy at the first of these, Aravon, County Wicklow: seemingly the other children threw stones at him and he was obliged to take refuge in a tree so often that all its leaves fell off, for which he was sharply reprimanded by the headmaster in front of the whole school. His tormentors would cry: 'The Knight of Glin is a Bing Bong Bin, his helmet is tin and his sword is a pin! Yah boo sucks!' Being deposited at school by his great-aunt Lady Meath's coachman driving a pony cart each morning cannot have improved his standing with his fellow students, either.

But after that he seems to have fitted in well enough. In October 1948, he writes from his next school, King's Mead in Sussex: 'We have lost two matches this term, there are two more today I hope we win them.' This must have been just about the last time Desmond expressed any interest in sport. (Interviewed by *Hello!* magazine in July 1990, Desmond was asked if he enjoyed sport. His robust reply: 'Absolutely not. I've no interest in sports. My healthy colour comes probably from having a glass of wine at lunch.')

Desmond's father, despite repeated efforts to find a cure for his illness, finally died in April 1949. Like his ancestor the 24th Knight, Desmond now came into an impoverished inheritance at the age of twelve. Perhaps his academic troubles can be considered as due to grief at the loss of a parent. Yet even while his father was still alive he displayed consistent disinterest in study. After repeatedly failing to get into Eton he was sent to Stowe.

Founded in 1923 and occupying the former seat of the Dukes of Buckingham and Chandos in Buckinghamshire, Stowe had hitherto had as headmaster the charismatic J.F. Roxburgh, who once said he wanted to turn out young men who would be 'acceptable at a dance and invaluable in a shipwreck'. Unfortunately, he had retired the year before Desmond arrived and his successor Eric Reynolds is generally regarded as having performed less well in the position. Stowe in Desmond's time was perceived as somewhere for boys who, like himself, had for diverse reasons been unable to win a place in their first school of choice. Dick Temple, who was there at the same time, remembers, 'My understanding was that J.F. Roxburgh believed in turning out civilized gentlemen and that was the culture of Stowe still, partly because of the ambience, the environment, this fabulous parkland and house. It was called the "Country Club" by other schools.'

Although not in the same house, Robert Jocelyn was a contemporary of Desmond's at Stowe and like him travelled over from Ireland at the start of each term. 'In those days,' he remembers, 'Stowe was not the best of public schools. It had a poor headmaster (Mr Reynolds) and most of the staff were about average to say the best. What we did have was almost untrammelled freedom in wonderful surroundings. The grounds were nothing like they are today and many of the buildings were falling into serious decay.' Those buildings and the grounds in which they were set would leave a lasting mark on Desmond but little else about Stowe seems to have been to his taste. George Adams, another contemporary who was in the same house, Grenville, recalls, 'We had a very hard taskmaster in the form of our housemaster [Brian Gibson, known to the boys as "Slug"] who expected all to be as keen on sport as he was, which did not suit Desmond too well. He had a mass of blond curly hair and the handsome look of a Greek God and whether or not because of that he was teased a lot at Stowe.'

Desmond took refuge in the art school, where he drew and painted a great deal. His pen-and-ink drawings of the follies and temples of Stowe are extremely skilled and show an architect's eye for detail; they hang as a group at Glin today. He spent a lot of time in the library where, he later wrote, he occupied himself researching the various families into which his ancestors had married over the centuries: 'I still have a bound exercise book with these pedigrees and I must have been deemed a terrible little snob constantly delving into the fat volumes of *Burke's Peerage* and *Landed Gentry* in search of connections.' He was, says another of his contemporaries, Alan Spence,

> perfectly placed for his future career as his conversation down the dining table was always about houses and their disappearing demesnes (I think he could have written *Lost Demesnes* twenty years before its publication in '76!). He used to have long discussions on this with fellow Grenvillian

Count Zygmunt Zamoyski who had family losses of property in the Polish post-War II situation.

Many of those who were at Stowe with Desmond describe him as being something of a loner, not much given to mixing with other boys aside from a few friends like Zygmunt Zamoyski (who would die exactly a year after Desmond). 'There was something compact and neat about his appearance,' says Dick Temple. 'His voice was a drawl which was one of his main characteristics, along with golden wavy hair and a genial bearing. And always this look of inner amusement.'

According to Robert Jocelyn, 'Desmond was most fortunate in studying history under the only inspiring master – an unusual character called Bill McElwee. He and his wife (Patience) held court in their house not far from Stowe. In fact, it was really a school within a school.' Bill and Patience McElwee lived in Vancouver Lodge, a house renowned for its untidiness. But the McElwees were also famous for the kindness and hospitality they extended to generations of boys, including Desmond, and evidently did a great deal to make his time at Stowe more enjoyable.

Perhaps encouraged by Bill McElwee, it was during the same period that Desmond started to write for publication albeit only within the covers of the school magazine *The Stoic*. It seems that his first published piece appeared in a special issue, *Natural History in Stowe*, which was produced in summer term 1953 and for which Desmond rather surprisingly wrote about bats, not a subject on which one might expect him to have much knowledge or interest. More predictably, for the summer 1955 issue of *The Stoic* he wrote an article on the Irish historian Charles O'Conor who, in the early nineteenth century, served as librarian at Stowe to the 1st Duke of Buckingham and Chandos.

By the time this piece appeared, Desmond had left Stowe and moved to Canada. Since his father's death in 1949, his mother had struggled to find enough money to keep the Glin estate running. Even while the 28th Knight was still alive, Veronica had assumed many responsibilities for the place, which, in the aftermath of the war, had become unprofitable. It would have been understandable if, like many of her contemporaries in similar circumstances in Ireland, she had taken the decision to sell up and return to England with her children; this was a course of action encouraged by her own mother. Yet Veronica remained at Glin, determined to pass on his family estate to her only son once he reached maturity. She raised chickens, and grew vegetables in the walled garden, which were sold to the transatlantic flying-boat terminal in nearby Foynes, as well as growing violets that were sent by train to be sold at Covent Garden market in London. The money made from these enterprises helped to pay Desmond's school fees. Veronica also sold Denver Public Library a panoramic view of Estes Park, Colorado, painted *c.* 1877 by German-American artist Albert Bierstadt. This had come to Glin from Adare Manor when Lady Rachel Wyndham-Quin married Desmond's grandfather and made in the region of £5000 in the late 1940s.

Efforts were made to let the house, preferably for a period of several years. This would have provided Veronica with a guaranteed income while ensuring Glin was occupied. The problem was that nobody seemed interested in renting a castle in west Limerick. Typically, an agent in Dublin wrote to Veronica in August 1951 noting that 'on looking over the advertising which has been carried out, I find that about £55 has been spent advertising the castle during the past three months with, as you know, no tangible results'. By 1953, Veronica found herself obliged to take in paying guests. While the majority of Desmond's friends found Veronica difficult, one has to admire her pluck in hanging on at Glin when many other women would have abandoned the struggle.

Luckily, she did not have to struggle for too much longer because in February 1954, Veronica, who in the years since 1949 had had several admirers, married for a second time. Her new husband was a wealthy Canadian widower twenty years her senior called Ray Milner, a lawyer who also sat on the boards of many of his country's most influential companies. He had first met Veronica in the United States in November 1944 when she and the 28th Knight were on their way to Arizona in a bid to improve the latter's health. The two had kept in touch and when Milner, who was widowed in November 1952, came to Europe just over a year later, he met Veronica again and soon proposed to her.

It was an unlikely but successful match, with little of the drama that had characterized Veronica's first marriage. At least part of her motivation for accepting Ray Milner's offer seems to have been financial; as Margaret Cadwaladr has noted, before the wedding Milner wrote to Veronica asking, 'How much do you owe & to whom?' But if she would be the beneficiary of his largesse, so too were Desmond and Glin. 'That's why I married Ray,' she once told Olda FitzGerald. 'Because I knew he'd be a wonderful father for Desmond.' Ray Milner was one of the most important people in Desmond's young life. He offered the stability that had previously been absent, not least by providing Veronica – and her son – with financial security. Veronica in turn grew more relaxed and less volatile, and this obviously had advantages for Desmond.

Most importantly, Ray Milner became a paternal presence, calm but authoritative, offering sound advice and support, intuitively recognizing what was right for Desmond at each stage of his development to adulthood. Sometimes he discreetly directed from behind the scenes; surviving letters show him making various arrangements for Desmond of which the latter would not have been aware at the time. On other occasions his help was more overt, not least in relation to ensuring Glin Castle's survival, as will be seen. For the rest of his life Desmond always spoke in admiring and appreciative tones of his stepfather, a man he came to know much better than he had his own father and who exercised a consistently positive influence on his upbringing.

Following her marriage, Veronica moved to Milner's home at Qualicum on the east coast of Vancouver Island where she created a spectacular garden over the following decades. Initially, Desmond remained at Stowe but the following spring it was decided he too should travel to Canada. His reports from Stowe were no better than had been their predecessors at prep school. Although eventually he would catch up with, and surpass, the majority of his contemporaries, academically Desmond was a late developer. By 1954, it was apparent he would have little chance of winning a place at either Oxford or Cambridge. Desmond's mother and stepfather therefore decided the best option was for him to try for a place in a Canadian university. Before doing so, however, he had to spend a few terms at another private boarding school, Trinity College School in Port Hope, Ontario, which was established in 1865. Even before he left Stowe, Desmond was warned that in his new school he would be expected to work harder than before; a letter sent during his final weeks in England complains, 'You did not tell me about the physics and chemistry. This all sounds so grim that I try not to think about it.'

Simultaneously changing school and country might seem a wrench, yet Desmond appears to have made the transition with ease. In fact, moving to Canada proved to be highly beneficial: from being a rather introverted adolescent aloof from his classmates and unable to engage with schoolwork, he became outgoing and much more interested in learning. Letters from Port Hope to his mother and Ray Milner show Desmond settling into his new environment without effort, and indeed quickly establishing himself in a circle of friends.

Spurred on by his stepfather, Desmond worked harder than hitherto and gained a place to study fine arts at the University of British Columbia in Vancouver. However, his results were not as good as he or his mother and Ray Milner had hoped. 'It is such a disappointment to me to hear that I only scraped through,' he wrote from the château de Bresse-sur-Grosne in Burgundy where he had been sent to stay with the de Murard family to improve his French. 'I really expected to do well in history and the two Englishes as I worked hard for them all and they were not terribly difficult, I thought.'

In any case, he did succeed in gaining a place at the university and while there seems to have taken full advantage of all the campus had to offer. Desmond made a strong impression on his college contemporaries. Barry Mawhinney, who would reconnect with Desmond decades later when he was appointed Canadian Ambassador to Ireland in 1994, remembers that impact: 'I, a callow youth from Nanaimo, certainly held him in awe. With his languid air, the slight hint of the *flâneur* and Churchillian cadence to his voice, who could not but be impressed.' That voice was often heard in public because Desmond became a stalwart of both the university debating society and an institution called the Model Parliament in which topics would be discussed and 'governments' elected. Barry Mawhinney says Desmond once made a tour-de-force speech at a Model Parliament meeting at the University of Washington in Seattle: 'The American co-eds were enthralled. He was such a peacock, had such an air and so eloquent.'

His love of attention now manifested itself, as on the occasion when he and a debating rival, Brian Smith, fought a duel on one of the university's main thorough-fares; dressed in white and in front of a large crowd, the two men threw rotten tomatoes at each other. In conformist Canada in the mid 1950s this was considered riotous behaviour. 'He had a Rabelaisian side,' says Mawhinney, 'and for many of us that was an extraordinary example of freedom of expression.' When the two men met again in the mid 1990s, 'Desmond had this gravitas, he certainly had become a man more soberly committed to things that engaged him. The contrast was so marked but that's not to denigrate the earlier persona: he brought colour and vitality to my undergraduate days.'

Desmond's freedom of expression displayed itself in his editing of a campus magazine, *The Raven*, which, as Mawhinney notes, 'had intellectual pretensions' and included such items as a poem by Desmond in the November 1958 issue entitled 'Des Esseintes and the Philistine'. Much of *The Raven*'s fare was standard stuff, but Desmond once published something radically different, which one of his contemporaries at UBC, Peter Hebb, remembers 'consisted of a brown manila envelope stuffed with every poem, short story or squib printed on a different texture of paper, each a different colour and size, and with a different font, also with different colours.'

Overall, Desmond seems to have fitted into Canadian university life with aplomb while retaining his own memorable character. The only time he faltered during his three years as an undergraduate was when he was sent to the Canadian Officers' Training Corps at Camp Borden in Ontario. Barry Mawhinney, who was part of the same group, remembers that Desmond 'had an ill-fitting uniform, I think he wore a beret'. But it wasn't just the uniform that failed to fit. 'He didn't stay long,' says Mawhinney, 'I think he decided after a few weeks that army life wasn't for him and left.'

After graduating from UBC in 1959, Desmond was awarded a one-year international exchange scholarship by the World University Service that allowed him to work at the University of Malaya with free tuition, board and expenses. He flourished during his year in South-East Asia, as a succession of surviving letters reveals. For the first time ever he was on his own for an extended length of time, free to make his own decisions, go where he chose and do what he wanted. In addition, he was exposed to different cultures: it was an extremely formative time as he absorbed new sights, ideas and outlooks, and it proved to be one of the most decisive, and happiest, periods in his life. He made friends with artists, ceramicists, writers, politicians, professors, dancers, collectors and designers, as well as his beautiful fellow students. He would later say with pride and obvious pleasure at the memory that it was his far-eastern experiences that had lost him his boyish inhibitions.

Arriving in Singapore in June 1959, Desmond initially lived in university rooms but soon started to travel, setting off by boat at the start of August to explore Indonesia. From Jakarta he wrote to his mother, 'Well, this island is marvellous. Mountains, sea, temples and charming people. The whole place is chaos and trains, politics and time are just, if not more so, as incompetent, slow and impossible as Ireland.' A few weeks later he was in Bali and even more enamoured with what he saw:

> This place has surpassed all expectations. I think it must be one of the most beautiful places in the world … You know probably that I am not free with praise and hate superlatives and often have argued with you Mama about things being the most beautiful and the least, but the whole civilisation here is the most cultured in an unaffected and wonderful way that I have ever seen.

As he would do throughout the rest of his life, Desmond immersed himself in whatever environment he found himself and at the same time managed to become acquainted with the right people. So his letter from Bali continues, 'I am staying with a rajah in his palace. Things are primitive, no electric light or running water, but it is much more pleasant here than in the hotel in Denpasar.'

Once more in Singapore at the end of September he was able to report, 'Looking back on the last 2 months I can certainly say they have been the most interesting of my short life. I lived a charmed life from beginning to end, never having any difficulty, with red tape, military officials or customs.' So it continued during the rest of his time in Asia as he moved up through the Malaysian peninsula and into Thailand. From Bangkok in late December he wrote with rapture, 'Oh life is so utterly good these days. I am so enthusiastic I could jump off the balcony into the klong (canal) for joy. The sun is setting and the spires of the temples are glittering over the water while sampans and other river boats are busy on the river, chugging, gliding full of pineapples, fruit, rice and pots of indescribable oddities.'

In the New Year, he moved on to Hong Kong and from there to Japan, all the time relishing the experience and writing with gusto to Veronica and Ray Milner back in Canada. Throughout his travels he was picking up items for them, pieces of jewellery, porcelain bowls and vases, statues and carved jade, honing his eye as he travelled from one country to the next. He was also making notes on the buildings he saw en route and some of these were used for an article he wrote for the 1959 *Straits Times Annual*. One wonders how many of that publication's predominantly expat readership would have taken an interest in Desmond's thoughts on 'Palladio delineated, colonial architecture in Malaya'. On the other hand, he was more confident of a receptive audience two years later when his feature on 'Europe reflected in Siam' appeared in *Country Life*.

Already Desmond had decided that in future at least some of his time would be devoted to authorship. In London shortly before leaving for Asia, he had meetings with the editor of *Country Life* and with several publishers; letters to his mother indicate he planned to write a book, although the subject is never stated, perhaps something relating to Ireland and her historic houses like Glin? In July 1962, he informed his mother, 'I think George Weidenfeld is going to publish a book of mine on Irish buildings: most satisfactory.' Three years earlier he had advised her, 'I am writing a short book on Javanese and Balinese art for a Singapore publisher. I hope it will be printed – Java and Bali are full of antiquities and the dancing in Eastern Java and Bali is an everyday occurrence.' Neither of these projects ever came to fruition but both indicate the direction in which Desmond's interests and abilities were leading him. While travelling on his own over several months in Asia he was able to give thought to what he might do for a living. 'I know that paintings are my chief interest in life,' he told his mother in August, before noting, 'I had better marry a Miss Agnew and go into the picture dealing business.'

In October he advised:

> I am applying to Harvard and Yale to do an M.A. in architecture and art history. After that I may go on for my PhD. Or perhaps try to get a job in some field of related studies to Fine Arts. Perhaps in a Foundation, etc. It is of course difficult to say. Really I think I will not be penniless?! ... I do want to spend next summer in Ireland, Mama, starting this book. What do you think? I feel more and more the intense desire to do it and it is a job that could be to me intensely satisfying. Admittedly it would not be remunerative but if one has a field of research and does a good book, this is quite a plume for jobs in those fields I mentioned.

In April 1960, Desmond was informed that he had been awarded a place at Harvard to study for a master's degree in fine arts. He moved there in September 1960 and initially felt rather overwhelmed by what was expected of him. Never especially responsive to academic discipline, his year in South-East Asia had removed him from a university environment and he did not find it easy to reacclimatize. Yet he persisted and, after completing his master's in autumn 1961, Desmond began the PhD on Irish Palladianism (discussed in the later chapter 'The Conservationist'). At the same time he was given a teaching fellowship in the Fine Arts faculty. 'The teaching job I now have goes very well and I am thoroughly enjoying it,' he wrote in February 1962. 'I give 2 lectures every two weeks and mark all their papers, etc.'

Friends who remember Desmond at Harvard describe him as being fast and funny and very sociable. Editor and writer Nelson Aldrich was a few years older and after graduating from Harvard and travelling in Europe was working for *The Boston Globe*.

> I lived with my grandparents in very grand style out in Brookline, a suburb of Boston, and took my social life in Cambridge. Since I was born into that *couche sociale* I probably met Desmond on his rounds. He made it clear that any time I wanted to, I could crash at his apartment. Of course I did, but I didn't give up the three maids at Brookline and he would come out there a lot where he was a big hit with my grandmother.

Florence Phillips, daughter of a classics professor at Harvard, also knew Desmond during the same period and recalls, 'I thought him charming and a little feckless. He was great fun, he was haring around all the time, an incredible social butterfly, having a great good time with sophisticated people.' One of those people, says Nelson Aldrich, was the African-American Dorothy Dean – sometimes known as the black Dorothy Parker – who was also then a postgraduate in Harvard's Fine Arts faculty. Around the time Desmond returned to Ireland, she moved to New York where she briefly worked as *The New Yorker*'s first female fact checker and was also employed for an equally short period at *Vogue*. However, mostly she was renowned for her excoriating wit and her friendship with the likes of Andy Warhol (she appeared in a couple of his films) and photographer Robert Mapplethorpe.

According to Nelson Aldrich, it was in Desmond's relationship with Dorothy Dean, 'a very touching one that played out, I think, until she died – that he learned to love the farther shores of eccentricity, the tragic romance of decadence, and, not least, the value of having an amanuensis'. Aldrich proposes that 'at bottom – and not so far down as one might think – D. was a serious person, wholly mindful of the larger (national) significance of his aestheticism, of the objects, from furniture to pictures to buildings, that gave him delight, and of his power and responsibility to share that delight as widely as possible'. But that side of him was rarely seen at Harvard. As Florence Phillips observes, 'It was only when I found him again in Ireland that I realized he was a deeply serious person on lots of subjects.' Although often spotted dashing from party to party – a trait that never deserted him – 'Desmond was much more disciplined during those years than I was, or than were most of his friends,' says Nelson Aldrich.

> There was nothing sloppy about Desmond. He was very aware, in a way I certainly wasn't, that he was at a stage in life where the terrible decisions had to be made. You had to get married, find a vocation, make money, attend to the exigencies of life: he was thinking about these things when the rest of us weren't.

At the same time Desmond was able to enjoy himself, not least thanks to financial support from his stepfather. This permitted him to travel around mainland Europe during the summer vacations of 1961 and 1962, some of the first of these being spent in Vienna in order to study German before he moved on to France. In July 1962, he was in England and was taken by Mark Girouard to meet Evelyn Waugh who lived at Combe Florey in Somerset, a house that had once been home to Margaretta Maria Fraunceis Gwyn, wife of Desmond's ancestor Colonel John Bateman FitzGerald, 23rd Knight of Glin. 'Waugh now lives there surrounded by good wine and Victorian pictures writing his memoirs,' Desmond wrote to his mother. 'He remembered funnily enough Daddy quite well in Lancing. It was most interesting meeting him and he was very hospitable which usually I may say he is not.'

Mark Girouard remembers that when he and Desmond arrived at Combe Florey, their host announced:

> 'I'm sorry that I haven't got a man to take your bags to your rooms.' We stayed the one night and then Desmond and I went for a drive to look at something else. When we got back, Laura Waugh was standing on the steps and said, 'I'm afraid you boys have got to go' and so we slunk off.

The following month, Desmond sent a succession of letters and postcards to Canada chronicling a motoring holiday through France and Italy that took him to stay with such luminaries as irascible art collector Douglas Cooper at the château de Castille near Avignon, aesthete Harold Acton at La Pietra outside Florence and socialite Mona Bismarck at her villa on Capri. Ten years before, he had been an aloof and solitary schoolboy at Stowe; now he was making up for lost time.

Back in Harvard, Desmond fell in love. He had already had a number of girl-friends (a letter from Singapore written in November 1959 opens, 'I am so sorry for not having written for such a long time. I have just been recovering from a rather complicated affair with a Chinese girl here, hence the delay'), but this was more serious. The Frenchwoman he announced would shortly become his wife was called Lawrence Letitia Coeffin, known as Laure. She was the great-great-grand-daughter of Napoleon Bonaparte's niece Letitia who had married the Waterford politician Sir Thomas Wyse, although many of her children (including the man from whom Laure was descended) were the outcome of an affair with a British naval officer. 'I see everything very clearly,' he informed his mother and stepfather, both of them stunned by news of an impending marriage, 'and I am positive you will love her ... she has that wonderful golden personality, charm, easiness, lack of preten-sion yet beautiful self assurance that very few people have.' 'She was very beautiful,' confirms Nelson Aldrich, 'tall and slender and very well turned-out, and was nice enough but in that very chilly, slightly de haut en bas French way. She was literally crawling with admirers.'

Just as quickly as it had flared up, Desmond's passion for Laure Coeffin fizzled out for reasons that are unclear: one friend suggests he turned against the idea of marriage after his intended bride, on first sight of Glin Castle, declared it would make a wonderful ruin. Whatever the explanation, the end of the affair seems to have had the effect of turning him against Harvard. In late April he told his mother, 'Goodness though, I suddenly feel the wish to go back to live in England and Ireland again. I don't want to spend any more time in the U.S. at the moment.' A month later, he was renting a little house at the back of Leixlip Castle from Desmond and Mariga Guinness. Glin Castle, on which over the previous decade Ray Milner had lavished so much money to ensure its preservation, was not available since it was rented out; the tenants, New York financier Duncan Spencer and his family, only left in autumn 1964. In any case, because he was supposed to be working on his thesis, it was better for Desmond to be closer to Dublin, and indeed to England. Leixlip remained his base for the next two years, until he moved to London.

In September 1963, Desmond advised his mother:

> I am applying for a job in the Victoria & Albert Museum woodwork
> department. I thought this might be a good idea for a year or two. I don't
> have to take it even if I get it if you see what I mean. It would be a very
> good thing to have done I feel ... The interview is not until November.

Desmond had been encouraged to apply for a job at the Victoria and Albert Museum
by head of the woodwork department Hender Delves Molesworth; 'woodwork'
was the name given then to the institution's furniture division.

A year after Desmond joined the department in 1965, Molesworth was
succeeded by Peter Thornton with whom he enjoyed excellent relations. Ronald
Lightbown who worked at the V & A during the same period remembers that 'the
museum was far from being a fuddy-duddy place. After the war, people had come
back and the collection was unpacked, and the place redecorated. Molesworth was
a genial person; he used to address his assistants as "my children". Between him
and his number two, who then succeeded, Peter Thornton, furniture study was
put onto a proper basis.' For the greater part of Desmond's time at the museum,
its director was the notoriously intimidating John Pope-Hennessy but the two men
seem to have enjoyed excellent relations, perhaps because of their shared Irish
background. Desmond, says Ronald Lightbown, 'wouldn't necessarily have treated
Pope-Hennessy with silent reverence'.

'Peter Thornton was the amiable keeper,' Christopher Gibbs – tastemaker,
antiques dealer, leader of fashion and dear friend to Desmond all his life – has
recalled,

> and there was a team of colleagues that included John Hardy, later a
> fellow worker at Christie's, Gillian Wilson, later to become the queen
> of the Getty Museum, Colin Streeter whose sexual exploits intrigued
> him, and later Simon Jervis, in due course to direct the Fitzwilliam, and
> bearded gothic Clive Wainwright – 'When I ask Wainwright for a piece
> of information, weeks later he deposits it on my desk like a turd.' Trixie
> the team secretary and Gillian vied to brew his morning marmite and
> sew on his missing fly buttons. Sir John Pope-Hennessy was the august
> director, and Desmond would bypass keepers and directors, persuading
> the Pope to acquire treasures he'd discovered directly. Desmond also

loved to imitate the Pope's plummy yet querulous tones. Desmond did a great deal of work ferreting out the design antecedents of the Norfolk House music room, was continually looking at the influence of Juste-Aurèle Meissonier, which he detected in the most surprising places. And of course above all he initiated his colleagues into the wonders of Irish furniture.

Desmond's years in London were highly productive. Not only did he carry out his work at the V&A with due diligence (and write several short books for the museum) but he was also involved in producing other publications with collaborators like Maurice Craig and with organizing exhibitions such as that devoted to Irish portraiture, which he and Anne Crookshank co-curated in 1969. It is indicative of his reputation for hard work that within months of taking up a position at the V&A he was able to tell his mother he had been offered a job by the London antiques firm Mallett. He turned it down, explaining: 'Really, only just coming here it would have been an extremely bad idea to have taken it. I really feel I should stay here a few years and establish oneself before moving on – and there will always be other chances. Still it is nice to think of one being asked!'

At the same time, Desmond enjoyed what can best be summarized as an extremely busy social life, much of it based around his second-floor flat on Pont Street. 'The rent is £600 per annum,' he told his mother in May 1965. 'This I feel is quite reasonable for the district and it is very light and the rooms well shaped. I shall let the smaller bedroom off to Paddy Rossmore who wants a pied-à-terre in London and he will only be there part of the time.' Sharing a flat with Desmond, Paddy Rossmore recalls, 'wasn't a great success. It wasn't a disaster, but we had very different lifestyles. He was much more social than I was, and had a lot more energy. He was always going out, up early in the morning, back late at night; I lived a more mousey, introverted life.'

Writing of Desmond in *Tatler* in June 2002, Tim Wills described him thus: 'He was a freezingly cool academic in the Beat years and a pivotal figure in swinging London, marrying or dating its steamiest sexpots and hanging out with pop stars and strung-out millionaires.'

Although somewhat hyperbolic, this representation of Desmond is not without an element of truth. 'London was swinging,' says Christopher Gibbs, 'and with it the Knight, so parties and late nights, wild dancing and hashish, an interest in altered states, swept up in an ever-widening social life, the shock and thrill of the new.'

Desmond's stamina now looks truly astonishing, he seems scarcely ever to have stayed still and yet somehow in the midst of so many distractions his work never suffered; he remained as industrious as his colleagues at the V & A while leading an extracurricular life they could scarcely imagine or hope to emulate. On the other hand, they were able to discover where he had been outside work hours since his name regularly appeared in newspaper gossip columns and in the pages of maga-zines like *Queen* and *Vogue*.

During his early days in London, Desmond's girlfriend was the beautiful model and actress Talitha Pol who had been born in Java; she married John Paul Getty Jr in December 1966. By then Desmond too was married. In late March 1966, he told his mother, 'I should love you to meet a girlfriend of mine who I think you might like for a change!! She is called Louise de la Falaise & is French. I am very much in love with her and vice versa. We do not however intend to get married for some time to make sure. So don't get in a flap!'

The daughter of French writer and publisher Alain, Comte de La Falaise, and his second wife Maxime, Loulou de la Falaise was a seventeen-year-old ballet student when she and Desmond first met but despite her youth was already causing a stir in London. She had strong Irish links: her maternal grandmother Rhoda Pike (whose husband, Loulou's grandfather, was the fashionable portrait artist Sir Oswald Birley), came from an old Quaker family in County Carlow, but Loulou had grown up between England, France, Switzerland and the United States, and was expelled from boarding schools in several of those countries. 'Then along came Loulou de La Falaise,' recalls Christopher Gibbs, 'the exquisite, the elegant, the most dandified of young women. Colleagues recall her visiting the museum, deranging Peter Thornton, clad in some glittering species of chainmail (Paco Rabanne?), the mesh very open and spangled with green jewels which failed to cover her bare nipples, no underwear (how do we know?), one cream, one violet stocking, and parti-coloured boots.'

By May, the couple were engaged and in October married in London with what one newspaper described as 'the most fascinating wedding of the year'. The day began with a religious service at St Mary's, Cadogan Street, the bride attended by eight children including the two offspring of Desmond and Mariga Guinness, Patrick and Marina; the groom's best man was the Hon. Garech Browne. This was followed by a reception for 300 guests at the St John's Wood home of the bride's grandmother Lady Birley, with a ball that evening at which Irish traditional musicians performed.

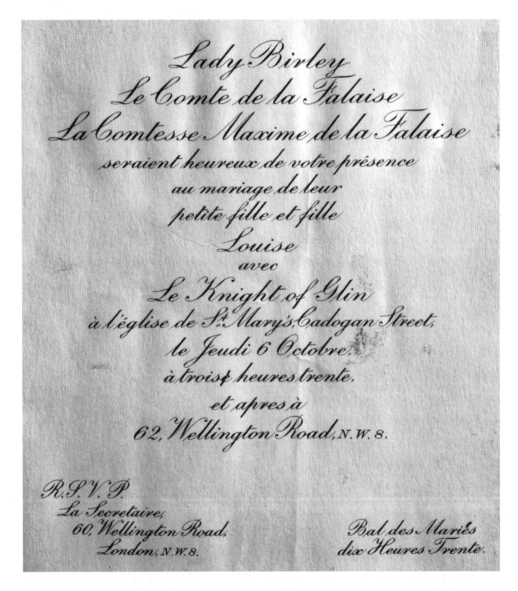

Lady Birley
Le Comte de la Falaise
La Comtesse Maxime de la Falaise
seraient heureux de votre présence
au mariage de leur
petite fille et fille
Louise
avec
Le Knight of Glin
à l'église de St Mary's, Cadogan Street,
le Jeudi 6 Octobre,
à trois heures trente,
et apres à
62, Wellington Road, N.W.8.

R.S.V.P.
La Secretaire,
60, Wellington Road,
London, N.W.8.

Bal des Mariés
dix Heures Trente.

An invitation to the wedding of Desmond and Louise de la Falaise that took place in October 1966.

Following a honeymoon in Mexico and New York, the couple returned to London and married life but within eighteen months they had separated. 'They were a wonderful pair,' remembers Florence Phillips who with her husband Jack spent Christmas 1967 at Glin Castle. She describes Desmond and Loulou as being 'like kittens playing together, very beguiling and fun'. John Stefanidis remembers them as 'a golden couple' in London, and other friends speak of wonderful parties in the Pont Street flat where they lived and where they were photographed by Cecil Beaton for *Vogue*. At the time, that publication's features editor Polly Devlin described Loulou as giving 'the impression that she has just ground part of *la populace* under her foot …' 'Against the face of aristocratic tradition,' observed a feature on the couple in the February 1967 issue of *Harper's Bazaar*, 'the FitzGeralds are completely caught up in the pace of today.' It was a volatile, lively marriage: John Harris tells of being at a dinner where 'Loulou came in naked and danced the whole length of the dining table in front of us.'

Various reasons are proffered why the relationship came to an end but the most obvious is that Desmond and Loulou quickly discovered they were incompatible. Despite his sociability, he was committed to scholarship, to learning more about Ireland's cultural heritage and to proselytizing on its behalf. In addition, he wanted – and needed – to spend time at Glin. Ireland and the role of chatelaine of a remote country house overlooking the Shannon estuary proved not to Loulou's taste. 'I suddenly found myself landed with the job of being hostess and I didn't like it,' she told *W* magazine in July 1976. Glin was too isolated for her ('She used to go up a nearby hill and scream,' Desmond told Tim Willis of *The Times* in September 1990). Essentially urban, she was more engaged by the new than the old, by fashion (in London she got a job styling shoots for *Queen* and would later become an inspirational muse for Yves St Laurent) and by the ever-shifting mood of cosmopolitan society. She was also very young when married to Desmond – eighteen at the time of their wedding, twenty when they separated – and had not yet found her métier. The split was largely amicable: by July 1968 Desmond was able to write to his stepfather, 'I have seen a certain amount of Louise and we are on very good terms.' They continued to see each other after their respective second marriages, and she died only a few weeks after Desmond.

Desmond reverted to bachelorhood but not for long: within a year the *Daily*

Express' William Hickey column informed readers that he could 'usually be seen around London with attractive former deb Olda Willes'. Daughter of a London stockbroker of English and Dutch descent and an extremely cultivated half-American mother, Olda had attended Desmond's wedding to Loulou with the latter's uncle Mark Birley, and the two of them had long moved in the same circles in London. According to Christopher Gibbs:

> The Knight met Olda Willes at one of his cousin Cara Denman's parties. Cara, born Guest, was a Jungian analyst and a wonderful woman. Seeking to heal her depressive mathematician husband Peter, she kept open house weekly at their house off Cheyne Walk in Chelsea. Here there was a changing mix of high bohemia, beau monde, wayward hippydom, beauty and intellect, memorable gatherings for many. Here was Olda, so lovely, so warm, so affectionate, so witty, and the Knight was again in love, but with a fresh resolve, a deeper need, something new and stirring. How lucky he was when love after all the usual stops and starts blossomed into marriage.

Desmond and Loulou were divorced and soon afterwards, despite the reputation Olda says he possessed for being 'the wickedest man in London', she married him in August 1970. Over the next few years the couple had three daughters, Catherine, Nesta and Honor, 'those legendary sirens of the Shannon' as Christopher Gibbs has called them. It can be said without fear of contradiction that his second marriage was infinitely more successful than the first, that Desmond and Olda made an excellent, complementary pair and that more than anybody else she provided him with the sustained support he required in his many diverse endeavours. 'My wife, Olda, is the person who gets everything done around here,' Desmond told *Hello!* in July 1990, 'and my mother was exactly the same: they are both strong women … Oh, my wife is clever. I'm rather temperamental and she is extremely calm, but she can be determined and firm, so she can deal pretty satisfactorily with me.'

At no time was this more necessary than in 1975 when Desmond had a breakdown. 'All the time I'd known him before,' says Olda, 'he'd always been up, always working under incredible pressure – he liked living like that – working twenty-four hours a day, whizzing all the time. Suddenly he went into this deep, deep depression; he couldn't get up, he was very sad and quiet and said he felt he was a failure.'

What was the explanation for this sudden, unexpected collapse? According to Olda, financial worries were at least partly responsible: 'it was brought about by anxiety and pressure, really to do with money. One moment he'd no responsibilities, and the next he had me and the girls and Glin. I think it was all too much, really. He became overwhelmed, just couldn't cope with it, and all the time there was Glin in the background.' In addition, Desmond was increasingly unhappy at work. In 1973, John Pope-Hennessy had moved from the V & A to the British Museum and Desmond did not care for the new regime that followed his departure. He was considered for the directorship of the Wallace Collection but this did not happen, and that probably exacerbated his discontent at the V & A. 'I urged him not to go,' says Ronald Lightbown. 'I felt he contributed something to the place that the others didn't, that he would take away qualities that were useful.'

Desmond's mental health so deteriorated that it became impossible for him to stay. 'I remember coming in to see him in the museum,' says John Harris, 'and he would be sitting there in the dark.' Olda found a doctor who diagnosed manic depression. During a visit to Canada ('his mother just could not accept there was anything the matter with him') another doctor confirmed the diagnosis and so Desmond started to take the anti-mania medication Lithium. 'You have to be careful about the dosage,' says Olda, 'and it took a while but luckily it worked for him.' Desmond continued to take Lithium for the rest of his life, and for much of the time it kept his mood stable. Occasionally there were highs – during which he, the inveterate collector, was inclined to engage in wild spending sprees – and lows that could last for several months. He never made it a secret that he suffered from depression or that he needed Lithium to remain balanced. In press interviews he often spoke of his condition and of how sound diagnosis had enabled him to resume the full, busy life temporarily suspended by ill health. 'He was the first person I ever knew who was lyrical about Lithium,' says Florence Phillips. 'There is a terrible stigma attached to it,' said Desmond when speaking of his condition to an American journalist in 1996. 'I always feel it is important to speak openly about it because it might help somebody else who feels terrified by the ghastly problems involved with it.'

At the start of 1975, Desmond resigned from the V & A and in April 1975 he and Olda and their children moved to live at Glin. 'I knew he had to come back to

Ireland,' Olda explains. 'Someone who was so passionate about the country had to be there. At first he could hardly speak, he would just lie in bed. So I put him in the garden and made him plant beans. Then Jo Floyd [then chairman of Christie's] came to stay and in no time Desmond was the company's representative in Ireland.'

Of course, Olda FitzGerald is correct: to achieve all that he did over the next thirty years Desmond needed to live in Ireland. It is almost impossible to imagine he would have become so immersed in the activities considered over the following chapters had he remained in London. He might well have become director of one of that city's great cultural institutions, but this would have denied even someone with his stamina and curiosity the time to research and explore his own country's artistic heritage. Only by being based in Ireland was Desmond in a position to make the difference that he did through his research, his books, his advocacy, his passion. As will become apparent, just as much as he needed to be in Ireland, Ireland needed him to live here. If he benefitted from returning home, so too did the country.

The Art Historian

IN JUNE 1951, Desmond wrote to his mother from Stowe, his letter mostly concerned with plans for imminent summer holidays. In the midst of this discussion he added, 'I am enclosing a picture of Barbara Villiers, Duchess of Cleveland by Sir Peter Lely. I think the portrait of her at Adare is a copy.' Written a month before his fourteenth birthday, even allowing for the fact that through his grandmother he had family ties with Adare Manor (and that his mother was a Villiers), this observation shows remarkable precocity on Desmond's part. It is an instance of character and interests manifesting themselves at an exceptionally early age.

In addition, the June 1951 letter demonstrates how Desmond was already concerned with correct attribution, a trait again manifested in an undated letter sent at some point in autumn 1955 during his first term at Trinity College School, Ontario. Once more writing to his mother he comments, 'By the way, I think the picture of Lord Clarina is certainly a Gilbert Stuart, its style corresponds to many I have been looking at in an art book here. He practised in Dublin to get out of debt in about 1780, just the right time for Clarina, and did many Irish nobility and gentry.' This picture had recently been acquired by Desmond's mother from the first Lord Clarina's descendants of soon-after demolished Elm Park, County

Limerick. Now attributed to the Irish artist Robert Hunter, it hung in the dining room at Glin until sold by Christie's in May 2009.

Inevitably, Ireland would come to lie at the centre of Desmond's engagement with art, but there were a few early diversions. While touring County Clare in June 1959 he went to visit 'a painter friend of mine Barrie Cooke who paints in the Burren surprisingly good modern nudes and landscapes. I bought a portrait he did which I think you will like very much.' And later the same year when travelling around Indonesia, Desmond met the distinguished artist Affandi (1907–90) who painted his portrait in a distinctly bold, expressionist manner. 'He is a wonderful man and his painting is glorious,' Desmond wrote at the time, commenting of the portrait, 'For want of something better to liken it to I would say a mixture of Kokoschka and Van Gogh,' a fair assessment. (This picture was sold in the 2009 Glin sale.)

Even when buying old pictures during this period Desmond did not confine himself to those with an Irish connection. A letter he wrote to his mother in July 1959 mentions a sixteenth-century Italian painting he had picked up in London the previous month for £300 ('The dealer – highest references, I checked up with Agnews. Agnew also thought I made a good buy – was very pleasant, got £175 off!'). And two years later, he writes of paying a Mrs Grunsby in Cork £500 for a seventeenth-century Bolognese painting of David and Goliath. 'Colnaghi's offered me immediately £1,500 and the Ashmolean Museum, Oxford want to buy it too. I am not going to sell it till I find out more about who painted it, etc.'

Here were two sides of Desmond's personality, the wily dealer and the academic researcher, which happily co-existed throughout his life, much to the surprise of some observers who seemed to believe one was incompatible with the other. However, at this stage the researcher had the upper hand, not least when it came to Irish art. Around the time he quit Harvard and returned to Ireland, Desmond met for the first time a woman who would become one of his closest friends and collaborators, Anne Crookshank. There was already a connection between the two: Desmond's great-great-grandfather the 3rd Earl of Dunraven and Anne Crookshank's great-grand-aunt Margaret Stokes were both nineteenth-century antiquarians who had worked together investigating early Christian art in Ireland (after Lord Dunraven's death in 1871, Miss Stokes edited his three-volume *Notes on Irish Architecture*). This gave Desmond and Anne Crookshank a bond on which to build what was undoubtedly one of the most productive collaborations in Irish art history.

After spending time at the Tate Gallery and the Courtauld Institute, in 1957 Anne Crookshank had been offered the position of keeper of art in the Belfast Museum and Art Gallery (later the Ulster Museum). At the time, this institution owned startlingly few Irish pictures. In an amusing essay she and Desmond wrote for a Pyms Gallery catalogue in 2001, Crookshank recollected how on first moving to Belfast she had been conscious of her 'sad lack of knowledge of Irish painters of all periods' and found it a misfortune that she 'never knew the names of any of the artists whose pictures hung on the walls of the houses she visited'. Among those houses was Leixlip Castle where, as was so often the case, Desmond and Mariga Guinness introduced her to like-minded individuals, not least Desmond. In 1963, the two men together with Anne Crookshank and James White, then curator of the Dublin Municipal Gallery (he became director of the National Gallery of Ireland the following year), came up with the idea of organizing an exhibition of Irish pictures showing landscapes that included houses. The show was held in the Ulster Museum in June 1963 and in Dublin's Municipal Gallery in August of the same year. The previous May, having just settled into Leixlip, Desmond wrote to his mother:

> on arrival immediately started on the catalogue. We have got about 25 catalogue headings done. There still remain another 60. The introduction also has to be rewritten. We should have it all done by next Monday. Desmond [Guinness] and I go to Belfast tomorrow. Still it is interesting to do and Anne Cruikshank [sic] the Ulster Museum person is most efficient (Thank God!).

In 2001, Desmond and Anne Crookshank remembered that when they started working together,

> the extent of our ignorance was such that a panoramic view of Glin which we brightly described as J.H. Brocas, was discovered, after cleaning for the exhibition by Alexander Dunluce, to be signed and dated J.H. Mulcahy, 1839 – a Limerick painter of whom we had never heard. It was too late to reposition it in the catalogue under M. where it should have been. We were also very uncertain about two brothers called Thomas Roberts, we could not believe that two brothers would have the same

name, but we went along with Strickland, the bible of Irish art history, and five years later or even more, Edward McParland, the great Irish architectural historian, found the letter from Roberts' great-niece which told the story that Sautell Roberts took his brother's Christian name after his tragic early death.

At the time, the ignorance about Irish art to which the pair here confess was no greater than that of anybody else. Today monographs on individual painters and genres are regularly produced and Irish art history is widely taught in the country's schools and universities. This was far from being the case half a century ago. A great deal of academic research had been undertaken into artwork of all kinds produced during the Celtic era, and into whatever remained from the Anglo-Norman period. But the visual arts from the late seventeenth century onwards had been almost entirely ignored so that it was hard to believe painters and sculptors flourished in Ireland for 200-odd years before 1900. One suspects that at least in part this was due to an association in the public mind between much of these artists' work and the former British regime. The majority of paintings, drawings and sculptures of the pre-Independence era had been created for an affluent minority, as was the case everywhere else in Europe. But that minority's dominance had been overthrown and all manifestations of its former power cast into disrepute.

So even though the majority of artists working in Ireland were native to the country, their output was held in low esteem owing to associations with a displaced authority. The scant published material on this subject was inclined to judge Irish art of the eighteenth and nineteenth centuries as a provincial manifestation of what had appeared elsewhere during the same period. As Desmond told Renagh Holohan of *The Irish Times* in August 1981, 'I have rather zoned in on this Irish period because nobody else much bothered. They are the artefacts of the Anglo-Irish, if one can use that dreadful word, caste, so we have sympathy with them. In the beginning this was considered colonial, but they are as much part of our heritage as the Book of Kells.'

On the other hand, when Desmond began studying eighteenth- and nine-teenth-century Irish art it had received far less attention than the Book of Kells and other work of the earlier periods. The only significant source of information was the Strickland mentioned above. This was a two-volume *Dictionary of Irish Artists* published in 1913 and written by Walter Strickland, then registrar of the National

Gallery of Ireland. An alphabetical survey of all deceased artists known to have worked in Ireland, Strickland's work has been an incalculable boon ever since it first appeared. However, despite his diligence the book is by no means infallible and particulars are often given without a credited source. The quantity and quality of illustration is also decidedly meagre. On the other hand, in the absence of anything else, Strickland's *Dictionary* sustained interest in the subject over the next half-century. This was especially important because soon after the book appeared much source material was lost or dispersed, beginning with the destruction of the Royal Hibernian Academy during the Easter 1916 Rising. Thereafter, Irish art prior to the start of the twentieth century attracted little notice in print, a rare exception being Thomas Bodkin's *Four Irish Landscape Painters* (1920), two of whom worked in the eighteenth/nineteenth centuries.

Writing in the *Irish Arts Review* in 1988 of another eighteenth-century Irish painter James Latham, Anne Crookshank remembered how twenty years earlier when she and Desmond began their research for an exhibition of Irish portraits,

> one day in Trinity College, Dublin, I showed him a portrait of George Berkeley, bishop and philosopher, which I thought was of high quality, and which Strickland had identified from an engraving as being by James Latham. Strickland knew no other works by him and he was a totally forgotten artist. Desmond mused over it and then said, 'I know another painting by Latham, I used to look at it when I was a child and went to tea at the next-door neighbours in Tarbert. It's of two girls playing a harpsichord and I'm sure it's by the same hand' … Desmond was right. There was also another Latham in the house. Now we were well started and the search has gone on ever since. The search for documentary evidence has gone on too but that battle has been lost; every alleyway one tries to go down turns out to be a blank cul-de-sac and there is only one more known piece of documentation about Latham since Strickland's time, some three-quarters of a century ago.

In 1966, Anne Crookshank established the History of Art department at Trinity College Dublin, the first of its kind in an Irish university. Naturally, Irish art featured on the syllabus and this gave a spur to further research. Not long after taking up her position, she developed the idea of an exhibition of Irish portraits on which she and Desmond would collaborate. 'I had family portraits,' she says, 'and drafted in Desmond to help. I got quite a number of artists from Desmond Guinness as well because they'd both done some work in the south.' No such show had been held before, so devising a coherent presentation and coming up with a narrative that highlighted the merits of Irish artists was a considerable challenge, especially since both parties were still in the process of learning about their subject. When Anne Crookshank first met Desmond, 'he admitted that he knew nothing about Irish art. I agreed with him and said it was because none of us had been taught anything on the subject.' Finding and identifying suitable pictures was the first difficulty to overcome. *The Sunday Telegraph*'s Albany column in late March 1968 included an appeal from Desmond for owners of appropriate work to make themselves known to him: 'He is looking for pictures, preferably signed and dated, by such artists as Jervas, Slaughter, Hone, Hunter, Morphey, Hickey, Trotter and Archer Shee.' One wonders how many of these names were familiar to the newspaper's readership in Britain or Ireland.

Accompanied by a catalogue written by the two collaborators and featuring 115 pictures as well as some examples of sculpture, wax models and medals, 'Irish Portraits, 1660–1860' opened at the National Gallery of Ireland in August 1969. It then travelled to the National Portrait Gallery in London and the Ulster Museum in Belfast, running for almost two months in each venue. Writing in *Apollo* that autumn, Crookshank explained:

> We have identified a number of worthwhile painters whose standard is
> much higher than we expected and which equals all but the very best of
> contemporary painters in England. The truth is that in the eighteenth
> century, Ireland had more artists of quality than she could possibly employ
> and those who remained in Dublin were as good as those, like Hone and
> Barry, who made their careers in England.

Exhibition and catalogue alike called for a re-evaluation of Irish art leading to better awareness and appreciation of its qualities. But if the intention was to convince visitors that the artists on display were the equal of their contemporaries in other countries, the exhibition must be regarded as something of a disappointment. Even local critics were unconvinced. *The Irish Times*' Brian Fallon wondered did the show 'mean a turnover of the generally held opinion that this section of Irish art is rather mediocre and provincial? On the whole, I'm very much afraid it does not.' His view was echoed by reviews in England, Richard Ormond and John Kerslake writing in *The Burlington* that while the exhibition 'brings together a number of interesting but generally minor artists' the work they produced inclined 'to be sporadic and disconnected, and it is almost impossible to trace a continuous pattern'.

The *Evening Standard*'s Ian Dunlop was more generous in his appraisal, noting that one reason for inadequate appreciation of Irish artists was widespread misattribution: 'Many of their works have languished unrecognised under more fashionable British names: Lely, Hogarth, Ramsey, Highmore. For example, landscapes by the Irishman George Barret have been attributed to the better-known and more prestigious artist, Richard Wilson, and it has been automatically assumed that Barret was a much inferior painter.' Nevertheless, Dunlop concluded, 'The observation that the Irish have a genius with words but not with paint seems to remain unshaken.' On the other hand, there was universal praise for the catalogue and its authors, who were much lauded for their endeavours. Denys Sutton, editor of *Apollo*, wrote that the catalogue 'is a learned document containing much out-of-the-way information', while in *Country Life* John Cornforth considered the publication 'a foundation on which other people will be able to build'.

This was precisely the intent behind the duo's labours, although the first people to use the foundation they had provided would prove to be themselves. According to Anne Crookshank, the exhibition of Irish portraits 'really got Desmond going, it made him really interested when he discovered he didn't know who were the artists responsible for pictures he saw. We started looking at pictures together and discovering quite a few artists; it might take us some years to decide that a picture *was* Irish.' Around this time, an Irish publisher asked Anne Crookshank if she would be interested in writing a book on Irish art. 'When I told the Knight, he said, we can't do that, we've got to have a decent English publisher. So I said, okay, see if you can get a publisher, and he did, and that's how we started.'

The Painters of Ireland c. 1660–1920 was published in 1978. That it took so long to appear is partly due to the fact that both authors were otherwise fully employed at the time and therefore had to fit in their research as and when an opportunity presented itself. 'It was *such* a major thing,' says Anne Crookshank, 'such a big undertaking. If we hadn't done it together, it would have taken perhaps twenty years to have looked at all the pictures. We just wouldn't have been able, given we had jobs and were both very busy, to do it alone.' The absence of almost all documentary evidence meant the two authors frequently had to rely on their combined judgment to decide whether a picture was by an Irish artist. But first they needed to find the pictures. A lot of time was spent visiting public institutions and private houses, not only in Ireland but also in Britain where they knew there would be Irish pictures. As Anne Crookshank explains, 'We spent three whole days at Glin working out the number of houses we needed to write to; we just couldn't stop here in Ireland.' Having made their list and sent out letters of request,

> we tried to go to all the houses whose family had been sent to Ireland as viceroy, and they would have felt it was their job to appoint an Irish painter who made more of an effort for their English patrons. We began in Scotland and then went slowly down. I remember once we did five in one day, it was terribly hard work. We got a lot of pictures – but we saw an awful lot more.

In addition to families whose forbears would have had an official role in Ireland, there were also those who had left the country in the earlier decades of the twentieth century and taken pictures with them. 'I remember travelling on a train with Desmond,' says his former colleague at the Victoria and Albert Museum, Ronald Lightbown, 'and he had a large copy of *Burke's Landed Gentry of Ireland* which he was going through with a green pen; he always went to the addresses at the end to track down where material had gone.' Some of that material remained in private collections, some had gone to galleries and museums, all had to be investigated, assessed and deemed suitable for inclusion or not. While the search was extensive it could not be exhaustive. 'I think if we'd really gone to every house and gallery,' says Anne Crookshank, 'we would have found more Irish pictures. But we took this on when we were both fully employed and didn't have the time to go everywhere.' It was easier to cover all of the possibilities offered within Ireland, not least because the country was smaller. Anne Crookshank remembers Desmond 'would bring along his notes or ring me up and say you have to go and look at this picture'.

Throughout his life, Desmond was an indefatigable collector of scraps of paper containing information that might at some date be of use to him, or to someone else. With regard to the research he and Anne Crookshank undertook on Irish art over more than three decades, this material was subsequently given to Trinity College Dublin where it is now available for consultation in the TRIARC Centre. Browsing through the enormous collection of files, one quickly gains a sense of the pair's working methods, and also of Desmond's magpie-like habit of picking up snippets of potentially useful data. Among thousands of possible examples is a letter to his collaborator written from the V&A in late December 1969. This mentions a Scotsman who had called by with a poor-quality photograph showing a painting of one of his wife's ancestors, a follower of William III: 'The family papers show that he had his picture painted by one "Leatham".' Despite the bad reproduction, Desmond concluded: 'A very fine picture it is too, and undoubtedly strengthens all our ideas about Latham's oeuvre.' In the same file is a family tree, drawn by Desmond, in which he attempts to trace Latham's line from the mid seventeenth to early nineteenth centuries.

Interwoven with this accumulation of fragments, frequently written on whatever piece of paper first came to hand but then carefully placed into a relevant folder, are sheets torn from auction catalogues over several decades. Many of these likewise have notes scribbled on them as Desmond amends attributions or adds his own opinions to the accompanying text. Typically, a catalogue entry for the sale at Christie's in London of *The Windstorm* by Thomas Roberts in July 1989 is covered in Desmond's handwriting as he corrected what he evidently perceived to be infelicities. James Peill who collaborated with Desmond on another pioneering book on Irish furniture (2007) recalls, 'He'd been collecting photographs of Irish furniture for longer than I'd been alive. And he had an amazing collection of quotes and snippets that he'd been collecting for years and years.' The files at TRIARC also contain an abundance of index cards with further details, such as a note concerning the artist Robert Fagan, taken from a life of English sculptor Joseph Nollekens published in 1914: 'When the death of Deare the sculptor was communicated to Nollekens, he observed, "He's dead! Is he? The palavering fellow Fagan promised me some of his drawings but I never had any." ' Obviously, this anecdote had no direct bearing on Fagan's own output but it helped Desmond better to understand the painter's career, and to place him within the context of his era. It also gave him unprecedented knowledge of Irish artists' place within a broader European setting.

As for the process of compiling the text, at the end of their introduction to *Ireland's Painters* published in 2002 the two authors wrote: 'When we published *The Painters of Ireland* some critics commented on our conversational style and many people ask how we collaborate. Indeed it is by conversation, as we discuss each sentence and compare it together.' 'When collaboration is perfect – as theirs was,' comments Eddie McParland, 'neither is an amanuensis: both brought separate skills to a single task, and neither was more important than the other.' 'I sat at the type-writer,' Anne Crookshank remembers, 'and he'd start a sentence, and I'd finish it. The next one I'd start and he'd finish. We worked it out between us, we were in the same room the whole time.' The collaboration was not always easy. 'Oh, we often had tremendous disagreements. He'd rush out of the house and you'd see him running around Trinity like a hare. Then he'd come back and I'd be rather stiff about it, then we'd work it out. I have quite a temperament too, but we got on terribly well …'

Anne Crookshank also makes the point that Desmond's eye for works of art, already instinctively sound, was greatly refined by the process of hunting for Irish pictures. It was this intuitive eye, allied with ever-expanding first-hand knowledge and an exceptionally retentive memory, that allowed Desmond to become such a powerful advocate for previously neglected Irish art. Alan and Mary Hobart of the Pyms Gallery in London recall:

> One of the Knight's great skills was his instinctive feel for the different mannerisms which combine to make up an artist's 'hand'. He was a consummate connoisseur. At a glance he could tell you who had painted a picture. Desmond was sometimes perturbed by the lack of respect given to connoisseurship by younger art historians, but for him it was the foundation on which all art historical knowledge was based. A picture was brought into Christie's from an Irish house belonging to an American actor. Immediately Desmond knew it was by Thomas Roberts, the greatest of Irish landscape painters of the eighteenth century. The remarkable thing about this brilliant attribution was the fact that this painting was wholly unlike anything else by Roberts then known. It was a winter scene and Roberts' oeuvre was comprised then – and indeed now – exclusively of sun-filled landscapes. However, as soon as one was told it was by Roberts it was so utterly characteristic that one wondered how anyone had ever not come immediately to this conclusion. This is the art

of connoisseurship. Documentary evidence often supports the connoisseurial instinct and, lo and behold, in the catalogues of the Society of Artists in the 1760s was our picture entitled *The Frost Piece*.

Thanks to Desmond's attribution the Hobarts decided to pre-empt the picture going to auction and it is now in a private collection in Ireland.

Mistakes in attribution – surprisingly few – can be found in the first edition of *The Painters of Ireland* since the authors were dependent on an evolving knowledge of the subject backed by usually but not invariably sound instinct. They were conscious of the possibility of error. 'I sometimes felt we should have had more time to do a bit more research,' says Anne Crookshank.

> But Desmond said no, even if we give the wrong chap, the fact that we've mentioned him makes it worthwhile. I think this is very important: what we did was make a start. We've made our mistakes, of course we have, but it's because someone has come along and done more work. We never pretended it was marvellous: it's just that we started looking at Irish artists and got other people interested in the subject.

Even if there were sometimes mistakes and generalizations, and occasional over-reliance on not-altogether reliable sources, at least they had been brave enough to take on a neglected subject and for the first time present it for public assessment. Not everyone appreciated this. When *The Painters of Ireland* appeared, it was harshly reviewed by Bruce Arnold in *Magill* magazine where he noted that the authors

> cannot make up their minds whether there are two Thomas Bate paintings in existence or one. On page 31, Thomas Bate 'is known only by a single work', the Lord Coningsby portrait in the Ulster Museum. On page 53, they write of a Dublin view 'which can be dated 1699 from a study of the architecture included, and is by Thomas Bate'.

Arnold and other critics also felt too much attention was devoted to the circumstances in which art had been produced, and not enough to the art itself. It is understandable that this approach should have caused annoyance, and yet the two writers were right to tackle the subject in the way they did. In the introduction to the later *Ireland's Painters*, they quoted Ellis Waterhouse's description of *The Painters of Ireland* as 'a general survey on traditional lines' before explaining:

This is not because of any objections to the New Art History, but because we do not think this type of analysis can be attempted until a reasonable foundation of knowledge has been assembled. You need to know who the artists were, the society in which they lived and the patrons who bought their work. Irish history is not only hugely complex but also difficult to see behind the art of any period because of its wars, rebellions, violence, political undertones and even language problems.

Desmond always understood that before any proper evaluation of individuals or eras could be undertaken, there was need for a critical overview of Irish art's evolution after the tumultuous upheavals of the sixteenth and seventeenth centuries. As he and Anne Crookshank wrote in *The Painters of Ireland*, for a variety of social and political reasons there had been

> a total evaporation of the knowledge of the continuity of Irish artistic tradition back to c.1600 and beyond ...This collapse of knowledge has resulted in the few serious writers on Irish artists failing to find any comparable background against which to see their subject developing, and therefore automatically straining every nerve – often with little success – to slot them into a purely English scene. They have been so generally ignorant of even the names of Irish artists that they have succumbed to rather doubtful speculation rather than to research.

No one would dispute that by comparison with their predecessors, the research of Desmond and Anne Crookshank was extensive. Yet it often ended in cul-de-sacs. James Latham, the subject of Anne Crookshank's 1988 article in the *Irish Arts Review*, typified the difficulties they faced. When she and Desmond started investigating this artist, only one picture by his hand could be confirmed with confidence: a portrait of Bishop Berkeley in Trinity College of which an engraving also existed. A small amount of biographical information could be culled from Anthony Pasquin's *An Authentic History of the Professors of Painting, Sculpture and Architecture, who have practised in Ireland*, published in 1796. However, this racy book cannot be considered reliable since it appeared twelve years after the author (otherwise known as the satirist and poet John Williams) had been obliged to flee Ireland following the ill-advised composition of an attack on the administration of the Lord Lieutenant, the Duke of Rutland. Furthermore, despite Pasquin's positive attitude towards Latham, by the time *An Authentic History* appeared the artist had been dead for almost half a century and details of his career were already sketchy.

Thus when they came to assess Latham, Desmond and Anne Crookshank had perforce to rely on hunch and a slowly emerging awareness of his painterly mannerisms. In *The Painters of Ireland* they write of time spent in France, 'which we think probable … because he seems to have picked up elements of the style of several French artists, and he uses their mixture of realism and formality rather than the increasingly informal composition of English portraiture'. Especially when discussing attributions prior to the second half of the eighteenth century, the words 'probable' and 'may be' regularly appear in the text of *The Painters of Ireland*. The authors were doing something that had never been attempted before: presenting a chronological survey of painting in Ireland from the mid seventeenth to the early twentieth centuries, a period when the entire country was under the authority of the British government. In order to do so, and because specific information about artists was often not available, they had to rely on secondary references discovered in diaries and letters as well as contemporary newspapers and journals. Even material from these was relatively sparse, yet again throwing the pair back on their instincts.

The Painters of Ireland approaches its subject chronologically and within this framework individual chapters often focus on specific genres such as 'Portraiture 1750–1800' and 'Landscape Painters during the first half of the 19th century'. James Barry was given an entire chapter, while another discussed the careers of landscape artists George Petrie, James Arthur O'Connor and Francis Danby. The focus was not exclusively on Irish-born artists but, like Strickland before them, the authors paid attention to artists who had spent a reasonable quantity of time in Ireland such as John Astley and Gilbert Stuart. Irish artists who spent the greater part of their lives outside their native country and would therefore not be particularly well recalled there were also covered. In this way, those painters who remained at home and whose entire output was produced in Ireland were placed within the context of a fluid environment, one that seems always to have featured a number of artists passing through the country.

In this respect, Desmond's concern that *The Painters of Ireland* be published in England reflected the practice of many artists who appeared in the book. Like them, he was aware London offered access to a bigger market than would be the case if the work was handled by an Irish publisher. His ambition was to win admirers for the art of Ireland as much overseas as at home, and he had sufficient experience to know that a prophet is always better received in his home town if he has first attracted notice further afield.

Indeed, this proved to be the case, as *The Painters of Ireland* was widely reviewed, even if not always by critics with much knowledge of the subject. On the basis that somebody Irish is the best person to write about an Irish topic, *The Listener* gave *The Painters of Ireland* to novelist Edna O'Brien who pronounced it 'a delicious book to have'. In *The Guardian* another writer of fiction, William Trevor, decided the work was 'concerned with what was happening above stairs, while people, language, religion and culture were being smashed to pieces in the rainy Irish landscape'. Elsewhere there was more serious analysis of what Desmond and Anne Crookshank had done, the faults found in their labours not overlooked but the application duly acknowledged. At the close of a long review in *The Burlington*, Robin Hamlyn predicted: 'This is undoubtedly a book which will stimulate further research in several areas ... It is likely to remain a standard reference work for some considerable time.'

Meanwhile in *Books and Bookmen*, Douglas Cooper – never known for being easy to please (he grumbled that in this instance the typeface was too small for ease of reading) – considered the two authors 'deserve heartfelt thanks from all art historians concerned with the northern school of painting ... it is consoling to know a reliable work of reference regarding artists who worked in Ireland is always ready to hand.' This last comment was echoed in 2000 by Fintan Cullen in *Sources in Irish Art: A Reader*. Along with a number of curators at the National Gallery of Ireland, Desmond and Anne Crookshank, he wrote, 'have defined over the last quarter of a century, the most important artists and developments in Irish visual history from the seventeenth to the early twentieth century. Anne Crookshank and Desmond FitzGerald have established a canon which had been only tentatively suggested by such precursors as Anthony Pasquin and Walter Strickland.'

At the start of *The Painters of Ireland* the authors stated, 'We hope that this book may do something to dispel the rather negative opinions usually held about Irish painting.' Unquestionably, their ambition was realized as is evidenced by the steady rise in prices paid for Irish art from the mid 1980s onwards. There are few better indicators of interest in a work of art than the price it achieves on the open market. It is, of course, impossible to quantify just how much the labours of Desmond and Anne Crookshank were responsible for the higher sums Irish art thereafter made. But more information in the public domain and resultant greater awareness was certainly beneficial for Irish paintings coming up for sale. Prior to the publication of *The Painters of Ireland*, catalogue entries for eighteenth- and nineteenth-century Irish pictures offered at auction tended to feature little more than dimensions, provenance (where it was known) and perhaps a cautious attribution. Now for the first time there existed a resource on which to build something more substantial, and, not surprisingly, until the appearance of its successor the book was regularly cited in sale catalogues. It also stimulated still further research by members of staff, which, in turn, allowed auction houses to give prospective buyers more information than ever before about a painting on offer.

Naturally, there were other factors involved in this increased engagement with Irish art, not least the emergence of history-of-art courses, first at Trinity College under Anne Crookshank's professorship and then at other Irish universities. Graduates of these faculties started undertaking their own research into aspects of the subject and publishing the results. As one such talented graduate, William Laffan, wrote in his review of *Ireland's Painters 1600–1940* (an updated edition of *The Painters of Ireland*) carried by *The Art Newspaper* in December 2002, 'the fact that scholars of Irish art, so many of them Professor Crookshank's pupils, are in a position to suggest how their account of the subject could be amplified or corrected is in itself perhaps the greatest tribute to this remarkable pair of scholars without whose pioneering research the subject would still be very much a blank canvas.'

In their introduction to a Pyms Gallery catalogue, Anne Crookshank and Desmond wrote, 'The fact that Irish eighteenth-century paintings of quality are now fetching substantial sums in the auction rooms and in the fine art trade, is revealing as when objects are worth something they are usually given more serious study.' Today it is astonishing to consider what small sums were paid for Irish art even thirty years ago. In mid December 1988, *Dumas*, an oil by Jack Yeats dating from 1942, fetched £82,000 at an auction conducted by Taylor de Vere Smyth in Dublin. This price set a new record for any picture yet sold at public auction in the country. So remarkable was the sum considered that, in January 1989, *The Irish*

Times' Niall Fallon advised caution as 'it may be an isolated case'. On the contrary, the *Dumas* sale was an indication of what lay ahead. Exactly three years later, a new record for an Irish picture was set when Sir John Lavery's *Bridge at Grez* – long presumed lost until it had turned up in the United States in 1990 – was sold in London by the Fine Arts Society for £700,000; seven years later, it was back on the market and sold by Christie's for £1.32 million.

The latter sale took place in London, another indication of changing attitudes towards Irish art. Since the late 1980s, all major English auction houses had recognized that the Irish market had potential for growth and started to feature work from this country regularly in their sales. Christie's, of which Desmond was the representative in Ireland, held its first event devoted exclusively to Irish art in Dublin in 1988 and thereafter regularly ran such sales in that city as well as in Belfast. The other English houses preferred, as a rule, to offer Irish art in their London salesrooms, usually as part of a British sale. But in June 1995, Sotheby's organized an all-Irish auction at its London headquarters and achieved a total of £3.5 million, in itself the highest figure yet achieved at such an occasion. Competition from international auction houses encouraged domestic businesses to work harder if they were to survive and this also helped to develop the market.

In 2007, the three largest indigenous auction houses – Adam's, de Vere's and Whyte's – between them grossed some €31.7 million in art sales. This compared with €29.8 million in 2006 and, looking back further, a lowly €8.77 million in 2003. Likewise the two London auction businesses, Sotheby's and Christie's, had seen the sums realized at their annual Irish sales climb: from £5 million in 2005 to £6.1 million in 2007 for the former, and during the same period from £2.4 million to £4.4 million for the latter.

These impressive figures must be accompanied by two caveats. Since 2007, ongoing economic recession has seen the market for Irish art shrink. In addition, the highest prices have always been paid for twentieth-century paintings. For unfathomable reasons, eighteenth- and nineteenth-century art has never enjoyed the same vogue among Irish collectors and therefore never fared as well at auction. Nevertheless, after the publication of *The Painters of Ireland* prices paid for these pictures began to rise steadily. A house auction conducted at Powerscourt, County Wicklow, by Christie's and Hamilton & Hamilton in September 1984, saw George

Barret's *View of Powerscourt Waterfall* go for £21,600; when the same work came up at Christie's in London in November 2001, it sold for £207,250 – an almost tenfold increase in seventeen years. Similarly, Thomas Roberts' *The Sheet of Water at Carton Park, County Kildare* had been sold at Christie's in July 1983 for £62,640. Offered once more by the same auction house in May 2000 – again a gap of seventeen years – the picture exceeded its upper estimate of £150,000 to make £454,750, a price yet to be surpassed. Incidentally, that sale – which was devoted exclusively to Irish art – realized a total just shy of £6 million, which was likewise a record for the time.

Improved prices for Irish pictures meant more effort was made to discover and to research them. As a result, works that had long been forgotten or misattributed were now discovered not just in Ireland but in Britain and the United States, and even in Australia. While such paintings would have excited minimal interest prior to the late 1970s, now they warranted attention, especially once Ireland's economy started to pick up in the 1990s and created a new generation of affluent collectors. For the same reason, dealers started to consider it worthwhile mounting shows exclusively devoted to Irish art – both at home and overseas. When Alan and Mary Hobart established the Pyms Gallery in London in 1974,

> we were grappling with many of the same issues in the commercial world that Desmond and Anne Crookshank were engaging with academically … We were both concerned to establish the oeuvres and chronologies of half-forgotten artists and above all to fly the flag for Irish art. This, it might be added, was a much harder task in London of the seventies and eighties where IRA bombs seemed a monthly occurrence.

Desmond and Anne were likewise battling against prejudice and deserve credit for persistence. Furthermore, around the same time the Pyms Gallery began to host exhibitions devoted to what might be called Irish old masters, so too did Irish public institutions, not least the National Gallery of Ireland. In 1971, Desmond had been a member of the committee organizing a show of nineteenth-century Irish art at Cork's Crawford Municipal School of Art. In his introduction to the accompanying catalogue, Fr Cyril Barrett (a Jesuit priest who was a keen advocate of modern Irish art) noted 'this is the first major exhibition of Irish art covering the period 1800 to 1900'. That such should have been the case now appears truly remarkable but is indicative of how little interest even culturally informed Irish citizens showed in their national art history.

Again, at least in part, the explanation for this state of affairs must lie in the absence of available information. Understandably, Barrett therefore concluded the introduction with a plea 'that immediate and generous support be given to the scholarship which alone will enable us to appreciate our art treasures and prevent them from drifting abroad ...' The catalogue's bibliography provides evidence of how meagre were the sources available to scholars at the time. James Barry, who as mentioned would be the subject of an entire chapter in *The Painters of Ireland*, had been investigated in articles by Thomas Bodkin published in *Apollo* in December 1940 and January 1941, as well as in a Harvard dissertation in 1952. But for an artist as important as James Arthur O'Connor, further information seemingly could only be found in either Bodkin's *Four Irish Landscape Painters* (by then out of print for half a century) or in a feature on the artist published by the *Dublin Monthly Magazine* in April 1842.

Between the 1971 exhibition in Cork and the publication of *The Painters of Ireland*, a handful of exhibitions focusing on Irish artists were held, notably one devoted to Daniel Maclise at the National Gallery of Ireland in 1972 and another to Andrew Nicholl at the Ulster Museum the following year. But after the book's appearance, the number and scope of such shows increased: one thinks of 'Walter Osborne' at the NGI in 1983 and, at the same venue over the next two years, 'The Irish Impressionists in Ireland, France and Belgium' and 'James Arthur O'Connor'. These exhibitions were curated by young scholars (Jeanne Sheehy, Julian Campbell and John Hutchinson) and accompanied by catalogues that sought to assess their chosen subjects in a more meticulous fashion than had previously been attempted. The very fact that such events took place is another indication of a changing climate and steadily growing interest in the notion that Ireland possessed an art history worthy of consideration.

So too was the launch by Brian de Breffny of the *Irish Arts Review* in 1984, initially as a quarterly and then as an annual (it has since reverted to its original form). Beautifully produced and generously illustrated, this periodical also maintained high editorial standards, providing an outlet for research in the field of Irish art history that was getting underway in a number of universities and colleges.

As early as the second issue, for example, there were articles by Fintan Cullen on Hugh Douglas Hamilton's letters to Canova, and by Rosemary ffolliott on Frederick Buck. By this means, Irish art of the eighteenth and nineteenth centuries reached a broader audience than would have been the case had the articles been published in academic journals.

Desmond and Anne Crookshank deserve a generous measure of the credit for the change of climate that took place following the publication of *The Painters of Ireland*. One of that book's shortcomings was its focus on artists working in the medium of oil; watercolourists received scarcely any attention. This omission was noted and regretted at the time but was necessary as much for reasons of space as owing to lack of time to conduct the relevant research. But with the first book done, Desmond and Anne Crookshank decided to continue their collaboration, which saw the publication in 1994 of *The Watercolours of Ireland: Works on Paper in Pencil, Pastel and Paint, c. 1600–1914*.

Unlike its predecessor, this was not a book without precedent: in 1990 Patricia Butler had produced her survey, *Three Hundred Years of Irish Watercolours and Drawings*, which covered much the same territory as would Desmond and Anne Crookshank. But commonality of interest by no means negated either book; as has already been mentioned, one of Desmond's most attractive traits as a scholar was his eagerness for knowledge to be shared, especially when it related to a subject close to his heart. Butler's work should be seen not as conflicting but as complementing that being done by the two other writers. Given how little had been written on Irish art in earlier decades, every addition was to be welcomed.

Furthermore, Desmond and Anne Crookshank made no exaggerated claims for *The Watercolours of Ireland* or its contents. Their introduction began with a caution:

> At the outset it must be made quite clear, this book is not a study solely of masterpieces, there is no Irish J.R. Cozens, Girtin or Turner, but there are many visual delights in the works of George Barret, James Barralet, Francis Danby, Frederick William Burton, not to mention the ladies like Rose Barton and Mildred Anne Butler who dominate the late nineteenth century.

The main body of text likewise closes without grandiose assertions, the authors merely expressing the hope that their enterprise has indicated that art in Ireland moved on from no mean beginnings and has flourished ever since. Unlike England, Ireland produced no major masters of watercolour painting but a great many of the second rank who are too little-known, and who illustrate the natural beauties of our country. Many others who are virtually unknown throw a considerable light on the social life of Ireland over the last three centuries, and we hope the book may have unveiled many a surprise both in quality and subject matter.

Despite being launched with such modest aspirations, *The Watercolours of Ireland* met with universal approbation. Even before publication it had won the 1994 award for an art book from the Confédération Internationale des Négociants en Oeuvres d'Art, a deserved tribute to the two authors. Learning from the criticism fired at their first collaboration, they had taken more time over the work and, a frankly important feature, allowed more room for illustrations to accompany their text. In addition, over the intervening sixteen years they had opportunity to learn more, see more, ponder more. All this is reflected in the finished result. In *Country Life*, Huon Mallalieu welcomed this companion to *The Painters of Ireland* and judged it 'the better of the two – better organised and more readable'. The authors' acknowledgment in their introduction of Irish watercolours' limitations also helped them to win critical endorsement.

In *The Irish Times*, Brian Fallon observed that the book 'covered a prodigious amount of territory, some of it virtually uncharted' and also pointed out that 'What it does show, most unambiguously, is that there has been a considerable body of art works in Ireland in what are sometimes called the minor media.' Even Bruce Arnold, who had been so censorious of *The Painters of Ireland*, could offer nothing but praise for the new publication, writing in the *Irish Independent*:

> As one would expect from these two distinguished scholars of Irish art, their book is a rich and detailed study ... It is comprehensive, adopting a broad and catholic view in which the authors embrace drawing, in crayon, pencil, pastel, pen, as well as true watercolour painting; and it is historical, not in the obvious sense only, of presenting us with an historical narrative of periods and developments, but in placing greater emphasis on what artists did than how they did it.

The Watercolours of Ireland was never going to create as much of a stir as did *The Painters of Ireland*. As has been pointed out, much had changed since – and at least partly thanks to – the latter's publication. The quality of art produced in Ireland during the eighteenth/nineteenth centuries was by now much less of a revelation than had once been the case. It was more widely exhibited, the subject of greater study and of interest to more collectors. For that reason, the element of novelty was no longer present. Furthermore, the works this book examined – as Brian Fallon had pointed out, 'what are sometimes called the minor media' – have traditionally attracted a smaller following than oil paintings. But it was necessary for Desmond and Anne Crookshank to write *The Watercolours of Ireland*, to carry their research further and thereby to give a more complete view of artistic endeavour in Ireland from the late seventeenth century onwards than the first book alone would have provided.

In 1994, Huon Mallalieu had concluded his review of *The Watercolours of Ireland* with an expression of hope that the two authors 'will revise their earlier book – but will we live to see it?' Indeed he did. Desmond and Anne Crookshank now returned to the *The Painters of Ireland* and reassessed its contents. Quite rightly they concluded the moment had arrived for a new edition of their book, one that would take into account the wealth of material that had emerged since their first work. As Irish art rose in value, Desmond's position in Christie's helped him to discover and identify a number of paintings the existence of which had previously been unknown. Alan Hobart remembers meeting him in London on one occasion:

> He was bursting to tell me about a view of Dublin that he had recently identified as being by the incredibly rare eighteenth-century artist Joseph Tudor. 'You simply *must* look at it, Alan,' he enthused. A month or so later we did. Desmond pointed out the topographical details. The two cathedrals; Dr Steeven's Hospital; the Royal Hospital and far in the distance the obelisk on Killiney Head whose building in the 1740s helped pinpoint the exact date of the work. Knight's knowledge of Georgian Dublin was unparalleled. It was a masterclass in scholarly exposition. Moments later the stock room in Christie's fell dark, as the lights were switched off and Knight and I peered over the large canvas. One of the Christie's assistants slowly panned a torch over the painting as the evanescent blue light of Ultra Violet showed up the different layers which comprised the painting's surface; restoration has no hiding place from the implacable glare of UV.

The picture was in breathtaking condition; a week later we saw off stiff opposition to buy the picture for a client for close to half a million pounds.

The picture in question, Tudor's *View of the City of Dublin from the Phoenix Park*, was sold by Christie's in May 2002. Later that year, an image of the painting was reproduced in *Ireland's Painters 1600–1940*, the revised edition of the two collaborators' earlier work. In their introduction they observed:

> Well over twenty years has elapsed since the publication of *The Painters of Ireland* in 1978, and since then a great deal of new material has been published by colleagues and students, all friends. As a result we felt we should pool these resources and our own work into one volume and seek out more and often unknown illustrative material. It is surprising that new artists still appear on the horizon and new ground is constantly being broken.

As evidence of this new ground, one notes that whereas the original book only considered artists working in Ireland post-1660, the opening chapter of *Ireland's Painters* examines art in the sixteenth and early seventeenth centuries. The career of the aforementioned Joseph Tudor had been covered in the earlier book in two paragraphs: in the new book there are two pages devoted to him. By 2002, much more was known about James Latham whose life and work had been the object of interest to both authors for several decades. Now there is no mention of time spent in France, although the influence of contemporaneous French painting in Latham's portraiture is noted. For all the reasons already discussed, since 1978 so many more of his pictures had been identified that it had become possible to give a fuller account of the artist's life than had been the case in the first book.

This was true not just for Latham but for an abundance of other artists. For example, in *The Painters of Ireland* the authors had written, 'it is impossible to disentangle the artists of the Pope Stevens family. Little work by any of them is known, except for Justin.'

In the later book, on the other hand, two pages were given to the Pope Stevens family, including the attribution to Thomas Pope Stevens on stylistic grounds of several portraits for which the artist responsible was previously unknown. Again in 1978, Desmond and Anne Crookshank had mentioned William Turner de Lond, 'about who virtually nothing is known except that he exhibited fourteen pictures in Limerick in 1821'. By the time *Ireland's Painters* was published, however, a great deal more had been discovered about Turner de Lond, not least that the number of pictures he had exhibited in Limerick in 1821 was actually twenty-five, among them the splendid *George IV Entering Dublin* now in the collection of the National Gallery of Ireland.

However, as before, the authors did not make exaggerated claims for their subject, quoting artist and critic Brian O'Doherty's remark that Irish art is 'the gate lodge beside the big house of Irish writing'. 'This still remains true,' they wrote, 'but we hope that we have been able to push the squeaking hinges of the gate a little further open, so that we can see down the avenue with a better vision and notice the masterpieces that exist to tempt the eye further.' This desire was realized; without exception reviewers of the book commented that while Irish art had yet to produce a genius of global stature, it had been overlooked for far too long and deserved more international recognition.

Further research undertaken by a younger generation advanced the process. While Desmond and Anne Crookshank worked on *Ireland's Painters*, their efforts were being complemented by another pair of collaborators. In 2001, Nicola Figgis and Brendan Rooney published *Irish Paintings in the National Gallery of Ireland, Volume 1*. The first book to look at the institution's Irish holdings in depth, this magisterial work dealt with artists born prior to 1770 and was therefore built on material gathered for *The Painters of Ireland* three decades earlier. In their acknowledgments Figgis and Rooney wrote, 'We were extremely fortunate in being able to draw upon the scholarship of Anne Crookshank and Desmond FitzGerald, Knight of Glin, and occasionally worked in tandem with them as they compiled their new book on Irish painting. Anne and Desmond's enthusiasm for our project, and the generosity with which they imparted information and insight was an inspiration.'

The early years of the new millennium saw a considerable number of other exhibitions and catalogues appear: one thinks of the shows devoted to James Barry and Daniel Maclise, at Cork's Crawford Gallery in 2005 and 2008 respectively, as well as those on Hugh Douglas Hamilton (2008) and Thomas Roberts (2009) in the National Gallery of Ireland. Events of this kind would not have taken place without the groundwork undertaken over many years by Anne Crookshank and Desmond.

His own research continued apace, his connection with Christie's remaining beneficial to Irish art history. Around the time the text of *Ireland's Painters* was being finished, an album of drawings by Hugh Douglas Hamilton showing the poor of eighteenth-century Dublin turned up at a Christie's auction in Australia with the modest estimate of Aus$1000. In London, Alan Hobart remembers:

> We were immediately on the case. This was the Holy Grail for historians of the period. The urban poor were usually ignored, or at best marginalized, in eighteenth-century Irish art. Here, by contrast, they were depicted going about their lives in all its mundanity and hardship. We had a client for these in mind and had already booked our flights down under when word came that at Knight's insistence the album had been pulled from the sale. It was re-offered the following May in the Great Room at Christie's King Street.

At that auction, the volume carried a pre-sale estimate of £20,000–£30,000 but in the end was acquired by the Hobarts for a client for £193,650: 'We shook hands somewhat ruefully after the sale. The happy conclusion to this story is that within a year the *Cries of Dublin* had been published in a beautiful volume expertly edited by William Laffan – the great friend of ours and the Knight – and has subsequently been explored in more than twenty articles on Irish history and material culture.' It was typical of Desmond's ability to combine several of his enthusiasms that this publication, the costs of which were generously underwritten by a supporter, was sold to benefit the Irish Georgian Society (and images from the Hamilton folio were used as endpapers in *Ireland's Painters*).

The IGS's own scholarly journal, *Irish Architectural and Decorative Studies*, also provided an outlet for such material, another example of Desmond encouraging what might be termed cross-fertilization between his sundry interests. Published in 1999, the second volume carried an article by Philip McEvansonya on the eighteenth-century Irish pastellist John Warren's years in Bath as recorded in his letters. Similarly, Jane Fenlon wrote in the 2001 volume of Charles Jervas' time in Paris some eighty years earlier. Desmond's association with the Irish Georgian Society in turn benefitted his own research into Irish art; he would make the most of visits to the United States on behalf of the organization to visit galleries and museums that might, unbeknownst to them, own Irish pictures.

Above: Glin Castle, an abiding passion throughout Desmond's life.

Below: Desmond's father Desmond Wyndham Otho FitzGerald, 28th Knight of Glin, who loved motor cars and was known as 'the Nippy Knight'.

Desmond's mother Veronica Villiers (left), August 1928, at Kilruddery, County Wicklow, home of her future husband's aunt Aileen, Lady Meath.

Desmond's parents at the Limerick Hunt Races in 1930 when their marriage had yet to develop problems

An infant Desmond standing in front of the sundial in the garden at Glin and looking distinctly uncomfortable in the presence of the family dogs.

Desmond at Glin with his mother after his christening in July 1937.

Desmond aged two in the nursery at Glin where he saw more of his nanny than his parents.

Six-year-old Desmond lying on the grass at Glin; with Ireland isolated during the Second World War he led a solitary childhood.

Paddy Healy whose family had worked on the Glin estate for generations shared with young Desmond his knowledge of the region's history and folklore.

A photograph taken at Stowe while Desmond was a schoolboy there: he can be seen eighth from the right in the back ro

In the mid 1950s, the dilapidated fabric of Glin Castle was extensively restored thanks to the generosity of Desmond's Canadian stepfather Ray Milner.

Sixteen-year-old Desmond with his mother and stepfather Ray Milner on the occasion of their marriage in London in February 1954.

While at Stowe, Desmond developed both his interest in architecture and his drawing skills, as can be seen in this 1955 view of the house's library.

While an undergraduate, Desmond took part in a duel with one of his debating society rivals that involved the two men throwing rotten tomatoes at each other.

University of
Malaya

1960

After taking his degree, Desmond was awarded a one-year scholarship that allowed him to travel around South-East Asia and proved a happy and formative experience (as well as the only time he grew a beard).

*Desmond as a postgraduate student at Harvard where
he lived from 1960 to 1963.*

*The beautiful Lawrence Letitia Coeffin, known as Laure,
the great-great-granddaughter of Napoleon Bonaparte's
niece Letitia. In 1963, Desmond announced his intention
to marry her but the affair fizzled out later that year.*

To give just one example: in 1801 the Dublin Guild of Merchants commissioned a portrait from William Cuming of Charles Thorp, one of the city's most successful stuccadores who was then also its lord mayor. The picture depicts Thorp standing in the rotunda of the Royal Exchange (now City Hall) where he was responsible for the plasterwork.

Following the abolition of the Guild in 1840, its possessions were sold to finance the Merchant's School in Winetavern Street. Eventually, the portrait of Thorp came into the possession of Englishman Archibald Ramsden and was sold by him in February 1917 at Christie's in London for 180 guineas. The picture was subsequently acquired by the Ehrich Galleries in New York, and in turn sold to the Art Institute of Chicago in 1922 where it was catalogued as 'Portrait of an unknown Lord Mayor of London'. In 1995, Desmond correctly identified it as William Cuming's portrait of Charles Thorp.

Desmond's outstanding eye and memory have already been discussed here. As the Thorp portrait demonstrates, these assets, combined with his interests in history, genealogy, architecture, garden design and other related fields, provided him with the unique ability to identify not just the artist responsible for a painting but also its subject, and the context in which the work was produced. As a result Desmond was able to reclaim a large number of pictures for Irish art history and, where his own finances permitted, to purchase some of these for himself. For any collector, limited funds can be as much an asset as a drawback since they impose discipline and encourage the pursuit of items other more affluent buyers might overlook.

This was very much the case with Desmond's own approach to picture collecting. *Painting Ireland: Topographical Views from Glin Castle*, published by Churchill House Press in 2006, provided abundant evidence of Desmond's capacity to identify the merits of a picture most likely unapparent to other observers. Because his primary concern was not necessarily the place of the painter in the artistic pantheon or even in the calibre of a particular work but in what it represented, over the course of three decades Desmond had been able to gather together an outstanding group of pictures showing views of Ireland during the previous thirty years. Almost 200 examples from this collection were reproduced and discussed in *Painting Ireland*.

Edited by William Laffan and with contributions from fifteen art and architectural historians, the book can be read as a kind of festschrift to Desmond, an act of homage to his own outstanding scholarship. In *Painting Ireland*'s introduction, Laffan rightly commented of the topographical views at Glin that this was 'very much a scholar's collection', noting that while scholarship had influenced each of Desmond's acquisitions, 'equally the collection has informed the Knight's scholarship and his intimate knowledge of so many obscure artists'. One had fed the other. Laffan went on to note that the large number of collections of Irish art built up in recent years had been influenced by Desmond: 'If many of these collections surpass that at Glin in the sheer quality and quantity of the works included, few can match the scholarship, understanding of context and underlying sense of purpose evinced in the topographical works discussed below.'

More than forty years before *Painting Ireland*, Desmond had helped to organize the 1963 exhibition 'Irish Houses and Landscapes'. By 2006, the discipline of Irish art history, almost non-existent in the early 1960s, had become vibrant with activity, replete with scholarship, scrutiny and assessment. Again in his introduction to *Painting Ireland*, William Laffan noted that Desmond's approach to art history was 'based on correct attribution and the assembling of the oeuvres of individual artists and architects'. Today this fact-driven approach to the subject is regarded as unsatisfactory in many academic quarters: Professor Fintan Cullen dismissed it in 2005 as the 'preciosity associated with connoisseurship'.

Two responses can be made to that evaluation. In the first place, art history is as vulnerable to changing fashion as any other area of study and the present vogue for treating pictures as a class of socio-economic document may yet pass. More importantly, without the steady and determined investigation into Irish art history by scholars such as Desmond and Anne Crookshank, its evolution and development from the seventeenth century onwards, there could be no other sort of analysis. Facts must come first, interpretation follows later. As William Laffan remarked, before works of art can be subjected to critical analysis, 'it certainly helps to know who they are by and what they depict. Connoisseurship may be old fashioned, but there are fewer and fewer art historians who have the first-hand knowledge of so many different artists' styles to be able to separate individual hands and provide the hard core of facts on which further speculation must be grounded.' For so many of those facts in the realm of Irish art history we remain indebted to Desmond. He led; others may now follow.

The Conservationist

WHILE AT HARVARD in the early 1960s, Desmond began work on a PhD thesis, 'The Irish Palladians'. His supervisor was James S. Ackerman, Arthur Kingsley Porter Professor of Fine Arts, who has written extensively on both Palladio and Michelangelo. These two titans of architectural history have been the subject of extensive study ever since their own era but the same could not be said of practitioners in Ireland. Here, as in so many other fields, Desmond was something of a pioneer: when he embarked on his thesis architectural history in Ireland was not so much in its infancy as still awaiting conception.

As he wrote in 1962, 'Irish country houses have long been a neglected and bebrambled vista in the field of architectural history.' Desmond's self-appointed task was to clear away those brambles and reveal the sleeping beauty of Irish architecture to global approbation. Over the next five years there are references in his letters to the idea that the thesis be published as a book, as well as to occasional discussions with publishers in London about the project. The fruits of his research were not intended for academic eyes alone but for a broader audience. Thanks to his efforts, Ireland's place in the pantheon of architectural history would be immeasurably improved.

Published sources when he embarked on this mission were scarce. Between 1909 and 1913, the original Irish Georgian Society had produced five volumes of records, the first four dealing with buildings in Dublin, the last looking at a number of Irish country houses. Including photographs, sketches and measured drawings, they remain a priceless resource, especially since so many of the properties featured have subsequently disappeared. In 1915, Thomas Sadlier and Page Dickinson published *Georgian Mansions of Ireland*, a useful addition to the earlier books in cataloguing some of the country's most notable eighteenth- and early-nineteenth-century houses before the devastation that would befall them over the following decades. But the work of Sadlier and Dickinson, like many of those that followed, was as much concerned with Ireland's social history as with an assessment of her architectural heritage. Such is the case, for example, with Constantia Maxwell's *Dublin under the Georges* and *Country and Town in Ireland under the Georges* (1936 and 1940 respectively).

Almost from its inception in 1897, *Country Life* intermittently featured Irish houses, but usually only those already well known such as Russborough, County Wicklow, or Curraghmore, County Waterford. There was frequently an element of condescension in this publication's coverage, a suggestion that Irish architecture was of lesser value than that found elsewhere, not least in England. As quoted by Seán O'Reilly in his introduction to a 1998 selection of Irish houses featured in *Country Life*, Sir Lawrence Weaver in 1918 declared that 'the outstanding fact about Irish architecture is that, after the days of its round towers ... its poverty prevented the development of anything that can be called a native style'. The following year, when writing of the neoclassical interiors of Heywood, County Laois, Weaver decided these could 'only be called "Adam" if we admit a very wide generic use of the word', before noting 'a certain confusion of motif which is characteristic of Irish work of the period'. (Contrast this with Mark Girouard's observation in the same magazine in February 1964: 'There tends to be something a little impersonal about English plasterwork of the Adam period; Irish work of the same date, though often less sophisticated, has at its best a certain gaiety and freshness that has survived from the rococo period.') Not least because they usually only visited the country for a short period, until the 1960s *Country Life*'s writers did not engage in much serious research about the Irish houses on which they reported.

Ideal Irish Spot to Toast St. Pat

Knight at Harvard Would Rent Castle

LORD OF GLIN—Desmond Fitz-Gerald, who is seeking to rent his castle in County Limerick, Ireland.

HERE IS GLIN CASTLE, which Harvard graduate student wants to put up for rent. It has "40 or 50 rooms," six bathrooms and central heating.

By GLORIA NEGRI

Attention all Irishmen and adopted sons of Erin!

Should today make you yearn to see the spot where St. Patrick drove the snakes from the Emerald Isle, a Harvard man has the answer.

It's an 18th-century castle by the River Shannon that he wants to rent. It not only contains 40 or 50 rooms—he's not quite sure which — for toasting St. Patrick at a rollicking party, but it overlooks the spot where the saint became immortal.

Hard by Glin Castle is Scattery Island where St. Patrick preached and drove out the serpents. There are seven churches there now and a tower to commemorate the event.

The lord of the castle is a 23-year-old architectural student studying for his Ph D at Harvard. His name is Desmond John Villiers Fitz-Gerald. Back home, Fitz-Gerald is known as the knight of Glin—the 29th knight of Glin, to be exact.

"But I don't use my title elsewhere, Fitz-Gerald said.

Fitz-Gerald has suddenly become eminently popular because of an ad he ran in a national magazine to rent his castle. On first reading, it might sound like a gag, but the ad is very authentic. It is something quite unusual for Ireland, Fitz-Gerald claims, because it has central heating and six bathrooms.

The knight of Glin would like to rent his castle for a term of years. He will rent it to a family or individual — "just so long as they are pleasant people," Fitz-Gerald qualified, in a very pleasant tone of voice. He's not quoting a price.

The ad also mentions "six principal reception rooms with 18th century plasterwork, 12 bedrooms, servants' quarters, main electricity, 10 acres of garden, golf, fishing and rough shooting in vicinity."

Some 600 Acres

In all, the Glin estate comprises some 600 acres, 300 of which are in farming. The property has been in the Fitz-Gerald family for 800 years.

The ruins of the original Glin castle are still on the estate. There are also ruins of some 40 or 50 other castles, once owned by the Fitz-Gerald family, all over County Limerick.

The present knight of Glin came into ownership of Glin castle on the death of his father in 1949. His mother, since remarried, now lives in Canada; his two sisters live in London and Portugal.

"We are of that breed known as the Anglo-Irish," Fitz-Gerald winked. He admitted being a bit wary of taking in today's parade, "because my accent (very British) often makes people take me for British."

As it happens, Fitz-Gerald explained, he was born in London (of an English mother and Irish father), and is therefore a British subject; he pays his taxes in Ireland, because he owns property there, and is a Canadian immigrant. He spent five years there studying at the University of British Columbia and got a scholarship from there to teach at the University of Malaya.

That he did, and also took the opportunity during his year in the Far East to travel in Laos, Hong Kong, Thailand and Japan. Fitz-Gerald is bug on traveling and, even though he must spend part each year at Glin castle, it more or less a token visit, except for Summers when likes to entertain, shoot and fish there.

Doesn't Want to Sell!

He doesn't want to sell Glin castle, "because someday might retire there." Nor does he exclude the idea there might be a lady Glin, who will be just dying to get into the housekeeping chores of a 50-room home.

Fitz-Gerald said he had had replies to his ad from all over the States, London and elsewhere and even from a Hollywood film company.

Glin castle is fully furnished. However, the third floor of the main block—there is a two-story wing—is slightly unfinished. "The Irish gentry used to outbuild themselves," he said, "and ran out of money before they could finish the third floor." However, he added, "it is a great place to store apples."

Fitz-Gerald's home away from home for about the next three years will be Harvard. He lives in Perkins Hall on the campus right now, but

While at Harvard in March 1961, Desmond placed an advertisement in various American publications offering Glin Castle for rent: as a result he was widely interviewed by journalists, something that would be the norm for the next fifty years.

Meanwhile, within Ireland from 1947 the *Irish Tatler and Sketch* began carrying features on important houses (including Glin Castle, which appeared in the December 1949 issue); in the majority of instances both photographs and text were by the elderly Jesuit Fr Francis Browne who approached the task with empathy and intelligence. However, his understanding of architecture was limited and as a result once more this subject received relatively little attention.

An altogether different tone is struck by Maurice Craig's seminal *Dublin 1660–1860*, which first appeared in 1952 and continues to be an invaluable resource. Here for the first time was a work that did not simply offer lyrical descriptions of the city's buildings but actually analysed their design and assessed their worth. It comes as no surprise that Desmond and Maurice should have been friends or that they would collaborate on the first book to carry Desmond's name: *Ireland Observed, A Guide to the Buildings and Antiquities of Ireland* (1970). Maurice was not just a superlative scholar: he shared with Desmond an intuitive ability to assess a building's merits.

Just as importantly, he possessed an admirably fluid prose style. It is, therefore, understandable that his book on the golden age of Dublin should have become a standard work, but disappointing that its publication did not inspire a flood of emulators. On the other hand, it took thirteen years for the 2000 copies of the first edition to sell. Tellingly, Dr Edward McParland in the introduction to his 'Bibliography of Irish Architectural History', published by *Irish Historical Studies* in November 1988, called the 1950s the 'bleak decade' for research of this kind.

Perhaps precisely because they had so few articulate advocates, during the same period a shocking number of important houses both in Dublin and throughout the rest of the country were lost either through destruction or neglect, and with them almost always went the records chronicling their histories. Readers familiar with my history of the Irish Georgian Society (2008) will, I hope, excuse me if I reiterate here a point made in that work: while many important properties were destroyed during the War of Independence and Civil War in the early 1920s, even more were subsequently abandoned or pulled down by owners who lacked the funds to pay for the buildings' maintenance. Prior to the establishment of the IGS there was no organization offering support of any kind to those who found themselves responsible for the maintenance of an historic property, and successive governments in Ireland had neither money nor inclination to help. In fact, official hostility was sometimes explicit, particularly from the Land Commission, a statutory body charged with breaking up old estates and distributing land to farmers in small parcels. In 1946, for example, the commission offered for sale Hazelwood, a large Palladian house in County Sligo built in 1731 to the designs of Richard Castle, on condition that the new owner demolish the building, remove all materials and level the site. Somehow Hazlewood survived this peril and, having undergone further degradation and abuse over the intervening years, still stands albeit in poor condition.

Meanwhile, throughout this period local authority rates were deemed payable on any domestic building with a roof; accordingly, the removal of slates became widespread. An iniquitous tax system meant the highest rates were charged in poor counties like Leitrim, which had few inhabitants and poor land, and the lowest in more densely populated areas such as Kildare and Meath. In the years during which Desmond was growing up, some of Ireland's finest houses were lost, among them Lismore, County Cavan (attributed to Sir Edward Lovett Pearce); Mrs Delany's former home Delville in County Dublin; Mespil House in central Dublin; Dunsandle, County Galway; Dromore Castle, County Limerick; Tudenham, County Westmeath; and French Park, County Roscommon. Two rightly famous examples will illustrate what happened to many houses in this period.

In 1957, the Land Commission announced its intention to demolish Shanbally Castle, County Tipperary, the largest and finest house in Ireland designed by John Nash. Writing in the *Cork Examiner*, Professor Denis Gwynn condemned the state organization's actions as an 'act of vandalism' and asked, 'What conceivable justification can there be for incurring the great expense of demolishing this unique Irish mansion?' To no avail: soon afterwards Shanbally's roof was removed and its cut stone gradually broken up for use in road building. Two years later in 1959, after decades of struggling to maintain her eighteenth-century family home Bowen's Court, County Cork novelist Elizabeth Bowen, then aged sixty, decided to sell the property. The purchaser was a local farmer, Cornelius O'Keefe, who, Bowen was led to believe, would occupy the house with his own family. In fact, within a year the building had been demolished and the site cleared. It was in response to this widespread dissipation of the nation's architectural heritage that in 1958 the Hon. Desmond Guinness and his first wife Mariga established the Irish Georgian Society, an organization with which Desmond would have a long and significant association.

His own awakening to the importance and vulnerability of Ireland's architectural heritage started early. Growing up at Glin obviously played a part in developing his eye, as did travelling to and staying in other historic houses both in the immediate neighbourhood and elsewhere around the country. During those journeys he saw houses not unlike his own falling into decay, their roofs taken off, their walls left to tumble. All over the country, the inheritance of eighteenth- and early-nineteenth-century houses was being permitted to vanish into oblivion. It left a lasting mark on Desmond. In the December 1969 edition of *House & Garden*, he explained that as a child he had first explored the winding stairs of late-mediaeval Irish tower houses, 'steps in themselves that led one on to their architectural successors, those small evocative, four-square doll's-house-like Palladian houses secretly enclosed in beech-girt demesnes, demesnes guarded by marvellous hawthorn trees, ivy and meadow-sweet'. The inherent romanticism of these lines indicates that Desmond's engagement with the built environment was as much intuitive and emotional as intellectual.

As such, it was fuelled when he was still a boy by a handful of local enthusiasts who recognized his potential. Standish Stewart, who with his brother Barney had a chemist shop in Limerick city, was a keen amateur antiquarian and photographer of old houses. In 1988, Desmond wrote how some forty years earlier as a boy he had regularly visited Stewart's premises, 'relieved to get away from my mother who was left to her tedious shopping in the red-brick Georgian streets of the town. Stan would show me tantalising photographs of old houses and ruins and it was he who kindled in me a life-long interest in architecture.' Likewise Paddy Healy, estate carpenter at Glin, shared with Desmond his deep knowledge of the area's history and folklore. Stewart and Healy were not occupants of the Big House but people who, despite near-universal disinterest among their fellow countrymen about the fate of Ireland's architectural heritage, wanted to ensure that at least an awareness of what was being lost would pass to the next generation. 'Limerick had its fair share of old houses,' Desmond later remembered, 'and as soon as I could persuade anyone to drive me I would visit them in my holidays.'

He continued to do the same thing after being sent to school in England. According to John Cornforth writing in *Country Life* in June 1998, around this time Desmond discovered Batsford's admirable *British Heritage* series of books, of which the most important for him was Ralph Dutton's *The English Country House*, first published in 1935. Within a few years he was cycling around the English countryside to explore such buildings first-hand, and, Cornforth reported, salvaging fragments of wallpapers from the then abandoned Butleigh Court in Somerset (a house, incidentally, which had originally belonged to the Grenville cousins of the family responsible for building Stowe). A letter to his mother written from Sunningdale School, Berkshire, when he was aged eight includes a drawing of a two-storey house beside a copse of trees. The picture is, as one might expect, a rather crude representation but Desmond's draughtsmanship improved rapidly once he moved to Stowe, where contemporaries remember him spending a lot of time in the art school. The immense house in which a succession of major architects from Vanbrugh to Soane had been involved, as well as the surrounding parkland adorned with a multiplicity of temples, bridges and other garden structures, could not fail to stimulate an already awakened interest. 'I've always believed Stowe had a profound influence on Desmond,' says John Harris, 'the ambiance, the great house and all the temples.' Glin Castle contains a considerable collection of pen-and-ink drawings by Desmond dating from his time at the school. Rendered in thick dark lines and displaying a real talent for suggesting the spirit of buildings, stylistically these works are reminiscent of John Piper, then at the height of his popularity. A couple of the drawings were reproduced in the school magazine in March 1953 and December 1954.

The latter is indicative of Desmond's concern with historical accuracy since, as the picture caption explains, he has shown the entrance into Stowe's park not as it then looked but rather 'the view which was originally intended'. Other issues of *The Stoic* carry reports of school art exhibitions in which Desmond showed some of these drawings. On one occasion, the focus of his interest becomes apparent thanks to a comment from the publication's reviewer that 'he almost always spoilt his work by not taking as much care over his trees and background as over the building'. Visits to other historic houses in the surrounding area such as West Wycombe Park further helped Desmond's education in this field and encouraged him to be concerned with the fate of historic buildings back in Ireland.

'It would be wonderful if you could establish a sort of National Trust in Ireland, wouldn't it,' he wrote to his mother in an undated letter. Presumably this was before 1953, that being the year Tervoe, County Limerick – which in the same letter he declares 'is such a lovely house' – was demolished. Shortly before this occurred, Desmond somehow persuaded his mother to buy two marble chimney pieces from the building, and 'painted panels and plaster plaques were thrown in for nothing'. The chimney pieces were installed at Glin in the dining and morning rooms and proved excellent purchases since the former turned out to be by the eighteenth-century English sculptor Sir Henry Cheere (also responsible for the funerary monument to the 19th Earl of Kildare in Christ Church Cathedral, Dublin). Another piece, which came from Ballywilliam near Rathkeale, County Limerick, was also acquired and installed in the library.

As the above letter indicates, it was around the same time that Veronica FitzGerald started campaigning for the establishment of a National Trust for Ireland. Modelled on the lines of the existing National Trust in England, this organization would have ensured a future for large family houses such as Glin Castle. Veronica FitzGerald made great efforts to encourage support for her proposal, writing to Fr Browne: 'It occurs to me that you of all people would be the greatest possible help to the furtherance of keeping up the beautiful & historic houses in this country ...' She also involved a number of other people in the project, including Senators Edward McGuire and Frederick Summerfield, as well as Fianna Fáil deputy and former minister Patrick Little, first chairman of the recently established Arts Council. Ultimately, the proposal for an Irish National Trust came to naught, perhaps because Veronica, the driving force behind the idea, married her second husband Ray Milner in early 1954 and moved to Canada. It would be a long time before such an idea was resurrected with any success.

The loss of eighteenth-century buildings like Tervoe with which he had been familiar since childhood, and indeed the uncertainty surrounding Glin Castle's own future prior to his mother's marriage to Ray Milner, left their mark on Desmond. The preservation of Ireland's architectural heritage was not some abstract matter but of great personal interest. He was always conscious how precarious could be the fate of any historic property, especially once the original owners had left; in the case of Tervoe, for example, the Monsells, who had been there since the 1770s, moved out in 1951 and just two years later the house was gone. However, in the period after he moved to Canada to finish school and then attend university, not only was

Glin's immediate future made secure thanks to his stepfather but Desmond, away from Ireland for the greater part of every year, displayed less engagement with his native country than had been or would again be the case.

Desmond often said his first knowledge of the re-formed Irish Georgian Society's foundation was the news that he had been appointed to its first committee. At the time he was still an undergraduate at the University of British Columbia and would spend the following year travelling in Asia. Nevertheless, during the latter period he managed to produce his first article for the Society's *Bulletin*. Taking up the entire July–September issue, it dealt with a subject always close to his heart: the history of Glin. The text was preceded by another of Desmond's pen-and-ink drawings, this one indicating that Rex Whistler had replaced John Piper as an influence on his draughtsmanship. His second piece for the IGS *Bulletin* appeared in the October–December 1960 issue and examined Georgian Limerick, and country houses in the surrounding region; it shared space between the covers with an article by John Betjeman on landscape art.

Prior to his move to Harvard in 1960, Desmond spent the summer at Glin where he began to entertain some of the people who would thereafter be lifelong friends, not least because they shared his interest. A letter to his mother at the end of August reports, 'I have had a few people here on and off, which has been fun. Paddy Rossmore, the Guinnesses … My architectural friends the Harrises have just gone. Mark Girouard is here now.' All of the aforementioned would remain part of his circle of friends. Architectural historian Mark Girouard first encountered Desmond in London in 1959: 'We met through Neville Pearson [Sir Neville Pearson, publisher of *Country Life*], and we got on immediately because we had the same interests.' Then writing for *Country Life*, Girouard remembers that, after years away from Europe, Desmond 'knew very few people, but he was very quick at getting to know them. I certainly introduced him to a lot of people in the architectural world.'

Architectural historian and curator John Harris had come to know Desmond by this date; while still a schoolboy the latter had called in to the antiques premises in London run by Geoffrey Houghton Brown who employed Harris. As with Girouard, the friendship was instantaneous and lasting. Harris recalls an early trip he and Desmond took to see the eighteenth-century parkland at Painshill, Surrey (developed by Irish-born the Hon. Charles Hamilton), 'because I said that I'd been reading a book by [Finnish-born art historian] Osvald Sirén on the gardens of China and Europe in the eighteenth century.' This was the first of many such excursions they would make together, accompanied by Harris's wife Eileen (née Spiegel), following the couple's marriage in 1960. One of their generation's most distinguished architectural historians specializing in the work of Robert Adam, she would also become a good friend of Desmond. Yet despite first meeting and getting to know him in London, John Harris says, 'I think very early on I became aware of the importance of Ireland for Desmond.' In effect, he was using the knowledge acquired overseas to inform his understanding of historic buildings at home.

This knowledge would be put to good use once Desmond settled in Harvard in September 1960 and embarked on his doctoral thesis investigating Palladianism in Ireland. The text opens with an examination of buildings designed by Sir Edward Lovett Pearce (1699–1733) and covers subsequent architects working in Ireland up to and including Davis Ducart (died c. 1781), after which, Desmond wrote, 'the well-manicured fingers of the neo-classical designers clutched the whole island in their icy grip'. While this sentence leaves the reader in no doubt of his opinion of Irish neoclassicism, the same pithy – and presumably more favourable – précis of his attitude towards the country's Palladian architects does not exist: the contents page of a surviving manuscript indicates the thesis was to have a final chapter with conclusions but this does not appear to have been written.

Although never submitted, the thesis' research and preparation served Desmond well in further honing his eye and broadening his awareness of the development of Irish eighteenth-century architecture. Already in the April–September issue of the IGS *Bulletin* he was able to publish a piece on 'Architectural Books and "Palladianism" in Ireland' subtitled 'A Study of Three Eighteenth Century Houses'. The three buildings in question were Newberry Hall and Lodge Park, County Kildare, and Colganstown House, County Dublin, all of which later appeared in Maurice Craig's *Classic Irish Houses of the Middle Size*. Desmond's examination of this trio indicates his preparedness to look beyond the familiar great houses to those that would be far less known, especially half a century ago.

At the beginning of his text, he states the challenge facing him and later scholars who entered the same field: lack of primary source material. 'The problem of eighteenth century domestic architecture in Ireland is a knotty one,' he wrote, 'for very little engraved contemporary work was ever exclusively devoted to the subject ... Dates, architects' and builders' names are rarities in research on the subject and very few mansions have the documentation that their British counterparts so often possess.' It is worth remarking again on this chronic shortage of documentation on the subject of Irish eighteenth-century architecture, and the lack of interest in the subject when Desmond embarked on his thesis. One of the only ways in which he was able to uncover relevant information was by travelling around Ireland and looking at extant buildings. This he began to do after returning from Harvard in 1963 and moving into a little house tucked behind Leixlip Castle where Desmond and Mariga Guinness lived.

In mid September of that year he wrote to his mother: 'I have already found 7 new monuments to be attributed to the architect Richard Castle about whom the first half of my thesis deals.' Presumably, at least some of these putative Castle-designed monuments were discovered during Desmond's increasingly regular trips around Ireland. In 1962, after selling his unmanageably large family house, Rossmore Park in County Monaghan, Paddy Rossmore had moved to a flat in Dublin's Merrion Square:

> In a rather vague way I took up photography and learnt the basics from a fashion photographer. Then Desmond FitzGerald asked would I come with him to the west of Ireland and we photographed things there, follies and old buildings and so forth. When I showed Desmond the results he was rather pleased with what I'd done. Architecture wasn't at all my subject, I just photographed what I was told.

Nevertheless, Paddy Rossmore's archive of images of Irish buildings, now housed in the Irish Architectural Archive, is an invaluable resource as well as being a record of the journeys he made around the country in the 1960s with Desmond.

They were frequently accompanied by Mariga Guinness whose fervour for Ireland's architectural heritage was hard to resist. 'Mariga was a very powerful influence on Desmond,' says John Harris. 'In fact, I would say he responded to her enthusiasm. For example, you'd be drinking champagne at 11 o'clock at night and she would say, let's go off and view a building and so we'd all climb into a car and zoom off. Desmond was infected by Mariga and learnt to proselytise through her.' Paddy

Rossmore recalls how Desmond and he, along with Mariga Guinness, 'would career around Ireland. We would go up these drives and then, if the house wasn't right, we'd turn around and drive away and the Knight would shriek, "Failure house, failure!" '

These trips set a pattern that would persist for the next half-century, making Desmond forever after an indefatigable explorer of houses not just in Ireland but wherever he found himself. More immediately, they helped further to refine his eye for the idiosyncrasies of Irish architecture, as well as provide him with first-hand information for his thesis on Irish Palladianism. 'What I really enjoyed was being with him in Ireland in the early days when he was discovering all the time,' says Mark Girouard who by the early 1960s had begun to write for *Country Life*, producing a two-part series on Glin Castle for the magazine in February/March 1964. He also remembers the regular presence of Mariga Guinness on these voyages of youthful discovery, a period when Desmond, who had spent relatively little time in Ireland over the previous decade, was becoming familiar with his native country.

Ultimately, his thesis was never completed, for reasons that are not absolutely clear. 'He just got on to other things,' suggests Professor Anne Crookshank who first came to know Desmond during this period. 'He'd no interest in the thesis any more. It wasn't that he couldn't do it, he just wanted to get on with other things.' In 2006 Professor Roy Foster commented of Desmond:

> He isn't a professor, though if he had stayed at Harvard he would no doubt have become one. However, he would probably have published much less and much less excitingly, and we would not be in such great debt to him as we are … Desmond FitzGerald would not have been contained by a university department. By following his own furrow, he has contributed an enormous amount to Irish scholarship.

Still, one must wonder whether that contribution could have been made without Desmond's early academic training. For the rest of his life, he remained prodigiously productive even while seemingly at leisure. The habit was established around this time. For example, in August 1962 a letter to his mother written in Capri (he was staying with fashion icon and socialite Mona von Bismarck, described by him as 'really angelic, so cosy, amusing & knowledgeable about everything') reports that while in Rome a few days earlier,

Two very important unpublished letters turned up about the architect of Castletown, my most important thesis house – you remember we went there after Leixlip when you were over. Now the whole history of the house becomes clear, I won't bore you with it but essentially it is the design of Galilei (he designed S. John Lateran in Rome). All very exciting to me.

The following month, by now in Venice, he wrote again to tell his mother, 'When I got back to Rome I met my professor Ackerman and gave him 200 pages of typed thesis, I now await in trepidation for his comments which he will write to me after he has had a chance to read it.' Ackerman did respond, and his comments were initially praiseworthy. 'I am greatly impressed with what you have achieved,' he wrote to Desmond, 'you contribute more to the field than the great majority of authors whose work I have read in recent years. I am pleased that you have made yourself an energetic scholar, and obviously have caught the bug.' However, Ackerman had a number of valid criticisms to make of Desmond's text, not least his tendency to describe buildings 'in an excessively restricted way, more-or-less as if they were assemblages of motives, particularly of windows, frontispieces and portals'. Unless Desmond included greater analysis of structure and materials, together with a broader consideration of context, Ackerman warned, 'you will come up with a long version of a *Country Life* article rather than with a solid work of arch. history'. Ackerman went on to propose that perhaps the solution might be for Desmond to focus solely on Richard Castle and his work: 'It is a much more limited subject, and won't perhaps make a book, but if you plan to write a book on the subject at large, you could not do better than to deepen your criticism in one area as a preparation.'

Desmond chose not to follow this advice, although he did write an article on Richard Castle for the January–March 1964 issue of the IGS *Bulletin*. Over the next few years, he continued to work on the thesis as originally conceived but one has a sense that other interests started to demand more and more of his attention, especially after he moved to London and took up a position at the Victoria and Albert Museum. Around that time Ackerman wrote to him again, pointing out that the text still suffered from the same drawbacks ('you approach houses like decorative sources ... often I cannot visualize the building at all') but urging, 'For God's sake, finish it!' As late as December 1966, by which time Desmond was married for the first time and immersed in an intense social life, Ackerman continued to urge that the thesis be completed: 'My overall impression is of a most useful and exhaustive effort that deserves warm praise for thoroughness ...'

It remained unrealized and Desmond's papers relating to his thesis are now held by the Irish Architectural Archive. The text's contents have been superseded by subsequent research but his work remains important as an early attempt to catalogue and contextualize the work of Irish eighteenth-century architects when this was little appreciated. In addition, the research he undertook during the early 1960s, both investigating documentary sources and exploring houses throughout the country, would stand him in good stead over the coming decades and provide him with unparalleled first-hand knowledge. It also meant that in his commitment to architectural conservation, passion was backed by solid scholarship: Desmond could never be denounced as a dilettante. Furthermore, here as in other fields that engaged his interest, he was always keen to share his discoveries and to inspire later scholars entering the same area. Had he not undertaken his thesis, it is unlikely this would have been possible.

Although a book on Palladian architecture in Ireland, like his thesis, remained unrealized, by the mid 1960s Desmond had begun to write pieces on Irish houses for various publications, following the lead of his friend Mark Girouard and approaching the subject with a similar sympathy. The October 1966 issue of *Apollo*, for example, carried a long article on the eighteenth-century amateur architect Nathaniel Clements – with whose work English readers were unlikely to be familiar – and looked at a number of houses with which he is believed to be associated such as Colganstown, Lodge Park and Newberry Hall, all of them previously analysed by Desmond in both his thesis and the pages of the IGS *Bulletin*.

As so often, he used the opportunity of writing for *Apollo* to proselytize on behalf of Irish architecture's special merits, noting that hitherto it had been 'an almost totally neglected subject'. Desmond intended to rectify the situation, his prose in this instance being employed in a passionate advocacy of Clements' talents, not least because the country houses he designed were the propagation 'of an architectural idea born in sixteenth-century Italy which was apparently unique in Ireland in its great period of domestic building'. In this way, Desmond directly links Clements with Palladio: the houses featured in his *Apollo* article were presented not as manifestations of Georgian provincialism but as comparable with contemporaneous work elsewhere in Europe. In this context, one should also mention other articles he wrote during this period, on Francis Bindon for the IGS *Bulletin* in 1967 and two pieces on Davis Ducart published by *Country Life* that year.

At the same time, he found other means of increasing interest in and awareness of historic Irish architecture. In 1965, he and Maurice Craig worked together for the first time in selecting original eighteenth- and early-nineteenth-century drawings, and compiling the catalogue for an exhibition to mark the twenty-fifth anniversary of the Irish Architectural Records Association. The show travelled to venues in Dublin, Belfast and Armagh before going to London where it was hung in the rooms of the Royal Institute of British Architects on Portland Place. Writing in *Country Life* at the beginning of January 1966, Mark Girouard, already a convert to Irish architecture's qualities, wrote that the exhibition 'makes clear how architects in Ireland, and particularly in Dublin, relatively unhampered by the existence of earlier buildings, were enabled to produce public architecture on the grand scale, and rose nobly to their opportunities. And it leaves in no doubt the competence, richness and variety of Irish Georgian architecture as a whole, private as well as public.'

Although his job at the V & A kept him out of Ireland for much of the time from 1965 onwards, Desmond continued to be a keen supporter of the Irish Georgian Society, which launched a London Chapter with a party at the Royal Academy of Arts in November 1971. That occasion was organized by the late Elizabeth Green who for a year served as the Chapter's chairman. But in 1972, Desmond took on the position, inaugurating his appointment with a lecture at the Irish Club on Eaton Square on 'The Irish Interior in the 18th Century'. He remained chairman until his move to Ireland in 1975 but over the intervening period did much to encourage support for the organization, not least by hosting evenings in his own flat. Olda FitzGerald remembers 'the parties for the Irish Georgian Society were just terrific. Numbers used to swell up the stairs and burst into the flat: lots of people in those days had grown up in Ireland or their parents had moved from there. Desmond's ideas of catering were very minimal: there'd be this watery Irish stew and all these grand people.' Around this time, Desmond also started to assume a role he would play for the next forty-plus years: keen supporter of anyone who displayed an interest in subjects that also held his attention, not least Irish architecture. In his address at Desmond's funeral, Dr Edward McParland remembered how the two men had first met in the late 1960s in Maurice Craig's London flat. 'Maurice had invited the Knight to talk to me about the architect Francis Johnston. Desmond rushed in late, gave me great help, and rushed out again: true to form, he was on his way from one party to another.' Eddie McParland was beginning to research late-eighteenth/early-nineteenth-century Irish architecture and, he recalls, 'Desmond kept in touch with me. I remember visits to the V & A and going down to a dingy canteen for coffee. Academically we had quite a lot to do with each other; he was terribly interested in what I was doing and keen to help.'

Having already worked with Maurice Craig on the exhibition and catalogue marking the Irish Architectural Records Association quarter-century, Desmond embarked on another joint project with the same collaborator. Published in 1970, *Ireland Observed, A Guide to the Buildings and Antiquities of Ireland* is an alphabetical gazetteer and yet so much more, precisely because the book reflects a greater breadth of knowledge and appreciation than is usually brought to such enterprises. While unquestionably helpful as a guide for visitors to the country, it is also a plea, unarticulated yet explicit, for greater appreciation of Ireland's architectural heritage. 'The emphasis of our predecessors,' wrote the authors in their introduction, 'has usually been on historic significance, dynastic or political, or on beauty of natural setting, which is something different from the beauty of things made by man ... Even that monumental achievement, the *Shell Guide*, our debt to which is obvious and gladly acknowledged, is the work more of archaeologists and historians than of architecture fanciers.'

The book's superior qualities were recognized at the time. *The Sunday Times'* influential chief book reviewer Cyril Connolly described *Ireland Observed* as a 'labour of love, and one which I hope will run into many more editions with additions ... One could wish it three times the size.' Whatever about additions, the book did enjoy several further editions, a tribute to the two colleagues' efforts. And there were gratifying tributes paid to their work. England's future Poet Laureate John Betjeman, who had spent time in Ireland as British press attaché in the early 1940s and before then had written the not-dissimilar *Shell Guides to Cornwall and Devon*, wrote enthusiastically to Desmond, 'This must be the first non partisan book to be written on Irish architecture. It tells me a lot I don't know … I really know how difficult it is to be both informative & interesting. Your entries are both.'

Piquing readers' interest before providing them with abundant information on the subject under consideration was a feature of all Desmond's texts. His prose style is never drily academic but often highly personal, reflecting an ambition to win more disciples for whatever cause is being promoted. He also understood how to appeal to romantic sensibilities, as was the case with his next co-authored book, published in 1976. *Lost Demesnes: Irish Landscape Gardening 1660–1845* was written in conjunction with Edward Malins, an English Yeatsian scholar, horticultural author and long-time supporter of the Irish Georgian Society; the Society had already carried a number of his articles in its *Bulletin* such as 'Mrs Delaney and Landscaping in Ireland' (April–September 1968). The dates covered by *Lost Demesnes* permit this work to be regarded as the garden companion to Maurice Craig's earlier book on Dublin. And while landscape gardening might not seem to be an obvious subject for Desmond, the fact that the book featured many houses and demesne buildings, as well as relying on paintings, architectural drawings, plans and photographs for visual documentation, explains why he would have relished the project. Furthermore, by this time he and his wife Olda had begun tackling the gardens at Glin, which duly featured in the book and encouraged his personal interest.

Like the majority of Desmond's other books, *Lost Demesnes* is notable for breaking fresh ground. No equivalent historical survey of Irish landscape gardening had previously been undertaken and the authors were perforce obliged to examine a wide range of disparate source material, much of which had previously not been consulted. As with Ireland's great houses, so their surrounding gardens were subject to widespread destruction over the course of the twentieth century and with them had gone much irreplaceable documentation. The task Desmond and Edward Malins set themselves was challenging but not, as evidenced by the finished book, impossible. As its title indicates, the tone of *Lost Desmesnes* is elegiac; a lament for what has been lost.

At the same time, the authors emphasized those features that made the country's landscape gardening different from that found elsewhere. As they commented in their introduction, 'The Irish union of man-made landscape with innumerable natural loughs, rivers, mountains and sheltered harbours is an achievement unique in European art.' And at the close of the book they made a plea for better appreciation of and care for what has survived, arguing that

> it will require imagination and judgement on the park of the State, both
> aesthetic and horticultural, to adapt [historic demesnes] so that they do
> not lose those qualities which inspired the love and appreciation of visitors in the past ... If this book with its many photographs can show something of Ireland's past glories and the destruction that has ensued during
> the last eighty years, it may indicate to our legislators, whatever their
> politics, the necessity of not repeating the sins of our fathers. Then we
> would feel our study has been worthwhile.

As so often before and since, the country's legislators opted to remain unmoved by these entreaties, but others recognized the value of the authors' argument. In *The Irish Times*, James White, then director of the National Gallery of Ireland, used the opportunity of reviewing *Lost Demesnes* to make his own passionate appeal for the preservation of remaining historic parklands, warning that unless the government became actively involved, 'in a very few years almost every fine property in the country will have been broken up and divided ... The owners of the finest and most important demesnes must immediately be seen to be the custodians of cultural property which belongs to mankind.'

By the time *Lost Demesnes* appeared, Desmond had returned to live in Ireland and become involved with a number of organizations such as An Taisce and the Historic Irish Houses Association, as well as the Irish Georgian Society of which he was made vice-president. He became aware on a daily basis of the vulnerability of Ireland's architectural heritage; in the same year *Lost Demesnes* was published he was involved with Christie's in the sale at Malahide Castle's contents. This book, coupled with spending a greater amount of time at Glin, brought home to him more than ever that a building is more than just an assemblage of various architectural motifs – an approach for which he had been chastised by his thesis supervisor.

From the late 1970s onwards, in his writings, speeches and interviews, Desmond would link together Ireland's historic houses, their furnishings, pictures and parklands; he recognized that each of them was dependent on the others and the removal of any one upset the entire balance. The dispersal of Malahide Castle's historic contents in 1976 demonstrated that a building's preservation alone was insufficient if its distinctive character was to be retained. Unfortunately at this time Ireland's historic buildings, their contents and gardens, remained as much at risk as ever from the twin evils of hostility and disinterest. Too few of the country's citizens cared whether properties like Malahide retained their original contents or not. Persuading them that it did matter now became one of Desmond's major concerns.

At the time of the Malahide sale, Ireland was the only member state of the European Community without an official national buildings record. In response to this lacuna, 1976 saw the foundation of the Irish Architectural Archive, set up to provide a central resource for the study of Irish historic architecture through the collection of both photographic and documentary records as well as architectural drawings. Now director of the IAA, David Griffin first met Desmond in 1969 in the Dublin bookshop Hodges Figgis: 'We were both interested in Richard Castle, he was looking at a book and we just got talking.' Desmond was an early champion of the Archive's work and remained so for the rest of his life.

> He was incredibly supportive and helpful, always generous with informa-
> tion and always ready to acknowledge anyone who helped him. He would
> often bring us photographs or tell us about something if he couldn't get
> hold of a picture himself. He would come in to the Archive with a brief-
> case and a big bundle of files would come out of it and be given to us.

The IAA was established by Eddie McParland and Nicholas Robinson who a year later produced *Heritage at Risk*, a report on the future of historic houses, gardens and collections in the Irish state, and made recommendations on how best these could be preserved. Some of the proposals were subsequently implemented by successive governments not least Section 19 of the Finance Act 1982 (and subse-quent amendments), which enables owners of historic properties to make certain restoration and maintenance costs tax deductible provided they open their houses to the public for a certain number of days annually. However, even with such tax concessions the future of many heritage buildings remained uncertain, as was made plain by another report that appeared in 1985. Edited by Professor Kevin B. Nowlan and Lewis Cohessy, *Safeguarding Historic Houses* argued for the creation of an inde-pendent property-owning trust for Ireland's architectural heritage, in other words for something similar to the National Trust in Britain. This was much the same proposition as that made by Desmond's mother thirty years earlier and despite initial hopes that the scheme would come to fruition, it made little progress.

Reading of Desmond during the 1980s and beyond, one has the impression of a man increasingly frustrated that well-argued reports and well-intentioned schemes for the preservation of Ireland's architectural heritage were achieving so few results. Following the sale of Malahide Castle and its contents, a steady succession of similar events occurred over the next ten years, among the more notable being Adare Manor, County Limerick, in 1982; Luttrellstown Castle, County Dublin, in 1983; Oldbridge House, County Louth, in 1984; and Mount Juliet, County Kilkenny, in 1987. When the last of these came on the market following the departure of the McCalmont family, *Irish Times* columnist Kevin Myers fulminated:

> The day is not far ahead when the work of the Republic will be complete, and not a single country house stands in this State. The triumphs of the 18th century will have been obliterated ... And then we shall be the glory of all Europe – a country with no intermediate history between the triumphs of the Gael and the triumphs of the Gaelic revival.

Myers' anger was matched by Desmond's; in these years he made little effort to hide his irritation that so few seemed to care while so much was being lost. Over the previous twenty years little seemed to have changed in terms of public attitudes towards Ireland's architectural heritage. As early as 1981, he was speaking of the need for a National Trust-type organization in Ireland to preserve the country's historic properties; in August of that year he told Renagh Holohan of *The Irish Times*, 'I feel frightfully strongly that these houses, their parks and gardens are part of our heritage and they should be helped to be opened. Otherwise they will not be here in another generation. I see them slipping away all the time.'

As the sale of Adare Manor was taking place in June 1982, he spoke even more bluntly about the necessity for government intervention, telling a *Sunday Independent* reporter that politicians would not intervene to save the house and contents for the nation because they believed there were no electoral votes in such a decision: 'People I meet abroad who are aware of the situation have been staggered that the State here allowed the Manor to go with such disinterest.'

In May 1985 he told *The Field*, 'Over the past number of years, we have seen many of our heritage houses disintegrate, and their contents scattered. Looking forward to the next 20 or 30 years it seems unlikely that unless some very immediate remedial action is taken any will survive.'

In April 1989 he advised *The Sunday Telegraph*'s Walter Ellis that 'the Irish are not well-versed in the world of aesthetics ... The whole structure of our cultural background is being neglected. It's simply not being looked after – and yet the heritage is a large part of what people come to Ireland *for*.' And by October 1993, when Hugh Massingberd was writing of Desmond in *Town & Country*, his remaining shreds of tact and restraint had been shed, with the author describing him as 'an angry man' who declared:

> We don't deserve to have an architectural heritage in Ireland ... In recent years we have seen so many of our heritage houses disintegrated and their contents scattered due to harsh taxation and lack of government support. Today there are barely twenty left with their families and collections more or less intact. Unless some very immediate remedial action is taken, I doubt any will survive.

Long before that outburst, Desmond had already reached the conclusion that if any of those houses was to survive, something more radical than a carefully composed report was needed to capture public attention and encourage the necessary changes in legislation. In 1974, while he was still working there, the V&A had hosted an exhibition with the self-explanatory title, 'The Destruction of the Country House 1875–1975'. Among its rooms was one called the Hall of Destruction, decorated with falling columns and carrying images of the many buildings that had been lost forever over the previous century. The show caused a sensation in England and did much to alter public attitudes toward the country house, previously regarded in many circles as an unaffordable relic from another era. One of the organizers of the show was Desmond's friend John Harris who remembers, 'We had such a stand-up row because Desmond said, but why haven't you included Ireland? I told him it was because we had a great archival body of evidence which just didn't exist in Ireland.'

John Harris was right: the sheer quantity of documentary and photographic information available about Britain's lost houses could not be found in Ireland.

Here was yet another instance where insufficient information hampered efforts to argue the merits of the country's architectural heritage and to secure its future. The same problem had spurred Desmond into embarking on his thesis about Irish Palladianism.

Lack of awareness had similarly meant the majority of Irish citizens did not realize the scale of devastation that had taken place in their country since the start of the twentieth century. In order to bring the loss to their attention, Desmond decided to produce an Irish equivalent of the 1974 V&A exhibition. As had now become the norm, he did not embark on the venture alone but allied himself with like-minded individuals, in this instance David Griffin, and Nicholas Robinson who had co-authored the 1976 *Heritage at Risk* report. 'The initiative came from the Knight,' Griffin remembers. 'The book came first, and he raised the money for it.'

The book in question was *Vanishing Country Houses of Ireland*, which contained introductory essays by Nicholas Robinson and Desmond, the latter displaying the breadth of his reading on the subject by quoting countless authors on the topic of the Irish country house. The cumulative effect of Desmond's text was to leave readers in no doubt that even if the Irish of late had failed to appreciate their architectural heritage, its excellence had not gone unnoticed or unrecorded in the past. The greater part of the book is given over to an inventory compiled by David Griffin, which chronicled 574 private houses of note, county by county, which, despite the title, were not so much in the process of vanishing as already gone.

Sponsored by Christie's and by Irish property-investment company Rohan Group plc, *Vanishing Country Houses of Ireland* was intended to shock. This was not meant to be an indulgence in mournful nostalgia but a grim exercise in counting corpses. It was supposed to encourage anger rather than sorrow. To make sure such was the outcome, an exhibition devoted to showing what had been lost was held on the premises of the Royal Hibernian Academy in Dublin. 'The catalogue of destruction is almost endless,' wrote Frank McDonald in *The Irish Times*, 'and it's not confined to the incendiary activities of so-called patriots during the early 1920s. What's so depressing is that we're still at it, wasting a precious part of our heritage for reasons of profit.'

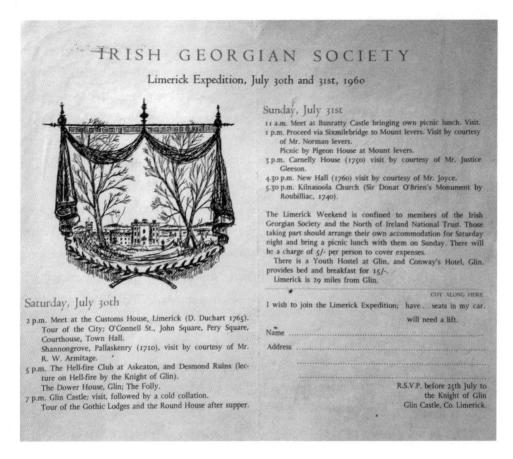

Desmond became involved with the Irish Georgian Society soon after its foundation in 1958;
two years later he organized a visit for members to houses in the Limerick region.

Anyone who visited the exhibition can attest to how dismaying were the images on display; how appalling their story of blight. And yet the occasion failed to cause quite the sensation expected. Although its tale was every bit as dreadful as that told by the V&A show, the Dublin exhibition did not have a comparable impact. Those already supportive of the cause of architectural heritage were horrified by what they found at the RHA gallery, those not engaged by the subject remained unperturbed. In fact, the show caused more of a stir outside Ireland. In February 1989, it opened in the London headquarters of Christie's. On that occasion, David Griffin remembers, 'There was a huge turnout, one of the largest ever at Christie's, they'd never seen anything like it.' The amount of publicity garnered in the English press was equally impressive, with large articles devoted to the ongoing destruction of Irish country houses. Reading these pieces more than thirty years later, one sometimes identifies a certain Schadenfreude; a smugness that while their country had come to recognize the importance of architectural heritage, the same could not be said of the Irish. Coinciding with a new expanded edition of Mark Bence-Jones' authoritative *Guide to Irish Country Houses* (which had first appeared ten years before), the *Vanishing Country Houses of Ireland* book and exhibition seemed to suggest that Ireland would soon have no historic buildings of note.

In a two-page feature in *The Daily Telegraph*, Hugh Montgomery-Massingberd called the exhibition 'a shocking catalogue of demolition and dereliction' and called for 'urgent action to stem the scandalous haemorrhage of the Irish heritage'. In *Country Life*, John Cornforth rebuked the Irish state for failing to pass legislation necessary to guarantee the security of what remained: 'Irish landscape, Irish ruins, Irish country houses have an intense romantic quality and are as crucial as Irish charm to the success of the country's tourism, but the romance has a price now way beyond private resources. The government should act now. Otherwise Ireland will see the strippings and demolitions, and the sales of contents accelerate in the 1990s.'

Both Montgomery-Massingberd and Cornforth were friends of Desmond and there is no doubt he did much to co-ordinate the barrage of publicity attending the exhibition in London, knowing that it would in turn be duly reported back in Ireland. Indeed, *The Irish Times* devoted two columns to advising on a denunciatory editorial in *Apollo* titled 'Alas for Irish Architecture'. Having regretted that Ireland had 'squandered much of its beauty through indifference, historical prejudice and lack of understanding', the editorial went on to warn that unless circumstances improved, 'in 20 or 30 years' time, the effect will not be at all different from what Ceaucescu is accomplishing in Rumania'.

Ironically, Nicolae Ceauşescu was to be overthrown and killed before the end of the year, but it took a little longer to effect real change in Ireland's attitude towards its architectural heritage. Nevertheless, letting the rest of the world know what was happening at home was a smart ploy on Desmond's part: no state likes to be the recipient of negative media coverage overseas. Even before the 'Vanishing Country Houses of Ireland' exhibition opened in New York in March 1989 – the first of a number of American cities in which it was shown – *The Irish Times* warned it would present a 'negative image' of the country with potentially harmful effects on the ever-important tourist industry.

In fact, for many years Desmond had been doing his best to entice more tourists to Ireland, not least because some of them came to stay at Glin Castle and thereby helped to make sure at least one Irish historic house remained in the hands of its original owners. But in addition, since the 1970s he had regularly travelled to the United States with Desmond Guinness in order to encourage support for the work of the Irish Georgian Society. At the time, no other organization in the country sought to awaken international interest in Ireland's architectural heritage, and to make non-nationals aware of the buildings they could help to preserve for future generations. From the mid 1960s onwards, first Desmond Guinness alone and then Desmond FitzGerald also made regular and repeated visits to the United States where their evangelizing speeches often won more converts and certainly inspired greater financial support than in Ireland. Without these two men's endeavours, the list of lost Irish historic houses would be longer and more dispiriting than it is today.

While both Desmonds were individually commendable ambassadors for Ireland, together they made an irresistible combination. As Christopher Gibbs has observed,

> Their hearts were in the same place, their gifts complementary, and the Knight, one of the earliest members of the Irish Georgian Society worked with [Desmond Guinness] for very many years. Annually they would storm America, relentlessly, successfully vamping the affluent with Irish antecedents, and their friends and supporters. The progresses of the two Desmonds and their outrageous blandishments (all for Ireland and architecture!) are legendary. They forged strong and enduring alliances to rescue and resurrect Ireland's great buildings, and to publish their researches. Of all organizations formed to save and honour old buildings the IGS is surely the merriest, the gayest, the most idiosyncratic and one of the most successful, a focus like Castletown for those who care about beauty and history, and spread their gospel.

Typical of the reception the two Desmonds received is the following extract from a report carried by the *Fort Lauderdale News* in March 1975, following their visit to Florida for a St Patrick's Day dinner in honour of the IGS: 'The two Desmonds who look enough alike (both handsome and debonair) to be a twin-brother, soft-shoe act, were a big hit with the membership. As you might expect.' Almost ten years later in February 1985, a rather more measured *New York Times* feature covered the pair's latest American visit on behalf of the Society and gave invaluable publicity to the organization's work. The piece pointed out that the IGS 'finds much of its patronage in the United States' and observed that 'both Mr Guinness and the Knight deplore the lack of support for their efforts at home'.

Nevertheless, the personal allure of the two men played its part in winning supporters for their cause. This was best exemplified by a 'Dinner with the Two Desmonds' held each autumn in New York for ten years from 1997 onwards. The brainchild of the IGS's then American executive director Arthur Prager, the occasion was invariably a financial success; the first dinner raised $10,000 for the Society. 'All the 120 participants were friends of one or other Desmond,' Prager later remembered, 'so it was more like an alumni reunion than a fundraiser.' The only problem was that everyone present wanted to sit next to the guests of honour, so 'in the end we worked out that the people who gave the largest donation got those seats'.

While much of their work on these trips involved being sociable and charming in the company of potential donors, there was always a strong pedagogic element as well. Desmond's scholarship combined with his first-hand knowledge of Ireland's historic architecture meant the talks he gave for the IGS were highly informative. Because he wished to instruct his audience in the intrinsic value of a subject close to his heart, he regularly participated in academic conferences and seminars in the United States. Among the earliest of these was a two-day event held at Pennsbury Manor, Philadelphia, in April 1971. Two years later, similar symposia took place in Boston and New York under the auspices of the IGS's local Chapters. There was a three-day seminar on Irish art and architecture in Washington in December 1979, and then in October 1981, thanks to Desmond's efforts, the New York offices of Christie's hosted a similar occasion for the IGS with an especially impressive line-up of speakers ranging from Kevin B. Nowlan on politics and culture in eighteenth-century Ireland to Anne Crookshank on Irish landscape painting and the Romantic movement. By such means, Desmond and the IGS sought to inculcate an appreciation of Ireland's cultural heritage overseas in the hope that eventually this would have an effect on policy makers back home.

In 1990, Desmond assumed a more central, more active role in the Irish Georgian Society. After thirty-two years at the helm, Desmond Guinness decided to retire as chairman and the following year as the organization's president. Both these positions were assumed by Desmond FitzGerald, who was the natural successor since he had been connected with the IGS since its earliest days and had already undertaken so much work on its behalf. One of his first tasks was to transfer the Society's office out of Leixlip Castle, in which it had hitherto been based but which was also Desmond Guinness's private residence, and into premises in central Dublin, first at 42 Merrion Square (courtesy of the Electricity Supply Board) and later at 74 Merrion Square. As an IGS newsletter in 1991 noted, 'The central location makes the Society more available to members and visitors alike and many people drop in to the offices ...'

While the newsletter continued to be a valuable way of keeping IGS members informed of developments within the organization, the *Bulletin*, published since 1958, was deemed in need of retirement. Accordingly, another innovation during Desmond's tenure as president was the advent of a new annual journal, *Irish Architectural and Decorative Studies*. Launched in 1998 to coincide with the fortieth anniversary of the IGS, *IADS* was at the time of its creation the only periodical dedicated to publishing new research on Ireland's architects and craftsmen. Its conception demonstrated Desmond's desire to encourage further research into subjects that had captured his interest so many years earlier, and to provide the sort of outlet not then available to him. Greater knowledge of Ireland's cultural heritage could only lead to better understanding and appreciation. As he wrote in his foreword to *IADS*, vol. VIII, 'The scrupulous scholarship this journal promotes, permeates and informs all aspects of our activities. It is a publication of which the society should be immensely proud.'

Better appreciation of the country's heritage grew steadily more necessary as the 1990s progressed and a building boom got underway across Ireland. Desmond was keen to make sure the IGS monitored planning applications throughout the country since many historic buildings were increasingly put at risk of either demolition for redevelopment or ill-considered alteration. In response to this new threat, the IGS appointed a planning officer, initially in a part-time capacity. Already in the autumn/winter 1994 IGS newsletter, Desmond could advise members: 'I am particularly pleased that the Society, through our planning officer Declan O'Leary, has made its voice heard on a number of occasions concerning detrimental planning applications.' Intervention grew still more important with the onset of the new millennium as much of the country became gripped by a seemingly insatiable appetite for new building, with ultimately detrimental results.

Desmond was not a hands-off president of the IGS. Constantly in contact with the organization's office and its staff, he was also very much a physical presence. Whenever in Dublin he could be found in the Merrion Square premises dealing with the never-ending correspondence (although he never got to grips with new technology and thus remained unable to use a computer). Letters, faxes and notes were sent forth in quantity, the majority looking for support of some kind or another for the IGS's work.

Typical is a letter to the editor of *Antiques Magazine* in New York in July 2001, and enclosing copies of the Society's *Irish Architectural and Decorative Studies*. 'I wonder if you can say something about them in your illustrious magazine,' enquired Desmond, never shy of engaging in flattery provided it achieved the desired result. Just as often, he was answering enquiries from concerned house owners or from people interested in learning more about specific historic buildings in Ireland. The quantity and quality of letters despatched by Desmond from the IGS's office is sufficient to fill an entire book and will no doubt be of use to the organization for many years hence. But certain threads run throughout his correspondence, not least an abiding concern that the future of Ireland's architectural heritage be secured.

The didactic streak in Desmond's character meant he wanted the IGS to instruct as well as counsel. Hence the project to produce a film about Ireland's country houses that would be both informative and engaging. Narrated by actress Anjelica Huston, who spent much of her childhood in Ireland, the eventual fifty-minute documentary contained interviews with a variety of well-informed sources such as writer Molly Keane, Desmond Guinness and Pyers O'Conor Nash of Clonalis, County Roscommon (ancestral home of the O'Conors, one-time High Kings of Ireland). Shown on RTÉ television on St Patrick's Day 1993, *The Irish Country House* set out to explain to the broadest possible audience the history and significance of these buildings and to argue for their preservation. This was not an instance of preaching to the already-converted but of seeking to attract new adherents.

It is, of course, impossible to assess the precise success of such an enterprise, but by this time – and despite Desmond's sometimes intemperate outbursts – there was a sense that the tide was turning and that the appreciation for Ireland's historic buildings he had so long sought might be coming about. Desmond was forever pros-elytizing for better awareness among politicians of the merits of Ireland's historic buildings. A conference on 'The Future of the Country House' held in February 1993 under the auspices of the IGS and another body, Irish Heritage Properties, was heavily oversubscribed. Even more importantly, the occasion was officially opened by Taoiseach Albert Reynolds who in his speech declared that Ireland's architecture of the previous three centuries had as important a position in the state's cultural and heritage policy as did the Neolithic, early-Christian or mediaeval. Mr Reynolds described as 'misguided' the latent hostility or bureaucratic and commercial indif-ference towards Georgian buildings that had been a characteristic of previous generations, and with regard to country houses declared the most efficient way to guarantee their protection and preservation was 'to help the owners as far as possible keep and maintain them and that this should be the basic policy objective'.

Even though this ambition was not realized in the short term, its expression by the head of an Irish government was unparalleled and demonstrated a change in official attitude. Nevertheless, more practical changes would also be required if the remaining stock of Irish country houses was to have a future. In a joint introduction to the conference's published proceedings, Desmond and Richard Wood warned:

> Unless the tangled skeins of tax relief are unknotted and rationalised and the will to help is fostered by government and other concerned bodies, Irish country houses, their gardens, parks and contents will soon be a fading memory ... We must not let the momentum generated by this conference die. It would be appalling if future generations could not cele-brate all aspects of their rich, diverse and varied heritage.

Desmond's valiant and persistent efforts on behalf of Ireland's architectural heritage now started to pay off. In January 2000, the government brought into law a new Planning and Development Act that addressed many of the concerns raised by Desmond and the IGS over previous decades. It was a significant advance in the protection of the national built heritage, with money allocated to all local authorities for the distribution of conservation grants within their areas and, even more importantly, for the provision of conservation officers within each authority. Other provisions ensured that, for example, owners of buildings listed for protection could no longer simply allow them to fall into ruin. However, owners who wanted to restore and refurbish their buildings still found the help provided insufficient, not least due to shortage of funds provided by the state for this purpose.

Within two years of the Act's implementation, the government had reduced funding to local authorities for conservation grants by 45 per cent, thereby undermining its own good intentions. As Desmond wrote in the IGS's summer 2004 newsletter, 'When one considers the number of local authorities in the country amongst which this sum is to be divided and then assesses the cost of undertaking repairs to a solitary leaky roof, it is clear that these funds cannot have any great impact on the actual requirements.'

On the other hand, thanks to the economic boom and appreciative new owners, some houses that looked as though they would have a precarious future instead underwent a resurgence: one thinks of houses such as Abbeyleix, County Laois, and Castletown Cox, County Kilkenny. Regrettably, many more historic properties lost their original character and appearance through ill-considered conversions into spa hotels and golf resorts, neither of which was likely to meet with Desmond's approval. In the early 2000s, he was asked to become a member of an advisory board assisting with the exemplary restoration of Ballyfin, County Laois, which today offers a deservedly lauded example of how an Irish country house can be impeccably refurbished and retain its spirit while at the same time becoming a commercial concern. This was precisely the kind of endeavour Desmond together with his wife Olda attempted to realize at Glin.

However, not everyone had the means, the ability or the interest to adopt such a course of action. State assistance to safeguard the country's remaining stock of historic houses continued to be the elusive goal. The ideal was the creation of an organization like Britain's National Trust, the kind of body for which Desmond's mother and then Desmond himself had campaigned tirelessly but without success over the previous half-century. Finally, in July 2006, such an agency appeared to have come into being with the official establishment of the Irish Heritage Trust, of which Desmond was one of the founder board members. The slow and tortuous process that led to the IHT's creation would take too long to describe here. There is no doubt that at first it seemed ideally placed to address many of the issues that had preoccupied Desmond over many decades, not least by providing a secure future for heritage properties that would otherwise be lost, despite the best intentions of their owners.

That this soon proved not to be the case was due to neither the IHT nor those behind its formation but instead to a combination of the global economic downturn and a failure on the part of the Irish state to provide expected financial resources. Desmond's wish that Ireland's remaining stock of country houses be preserved, an issue on which he had lobbied for many years, has yet to be granted. As he commented in an introduction to *The Irish Country House* (2010), 'The founding of the Irish Heritage Trust should have been a clarion call for the preservation of houses and estates whose owners could not afford to keep them going ... However, even this brief respite in the fortunes of the houses has taken a dramatic downturn.'

This was as public an expression of disappointment as Desmond allowed himself but it must have been a tough blow that the prize for which he had so long striven and which seemed to be tantalizingly within reach was snatched away at the last moment. 'He never talked about his disappointment,' says Desmond's daughter Catherine. 'He never got embittered, even after so much campaigning and battling. He did *so* much pro bono work it was unbelievable; so much of his life was unpaid. But he was such an optimist, he thought everything would work out for the best.'

Unfortunately, today Ireland's historic country houses together with their contents and parklands remain almost as vulnerable to the threat of dispersal and despoliation as they did when Desmond first began to explore them during his childhood. During the course of his life he fought long and hard to bring the glories of Irish architecture to the attention of as broad an audience as possible, both within Ireland and overseas. That he should not have seen an equivalent of the National Trust definitively established in his own country was a harsh blow.

It was fitting that *The Irish Country House*, like *Irish Furniture* co-authored with James Peill, should have been Desmond's last book, thereby concluding where he had started. The aforementioned introduction notes: 'The roll call of Irish country houses still in their original family's ownership has diminished to such an extent that desperate cries have gone out to save them before there are none left.' Nobody cried more desperately or repeatedly than Desmond, and if Ireland's architectural heritage remains imperilled, it is certainly not for want of effort on his part.

The Connoisseur

WRITING ON THE WEBSITE www.arthistorynews.com in February 2012, art historian and gallery director Dr Bendor Grosvenor discussed the vexed subject of connoisseurship. 'From about the late 1970s onwards,' he wrote,

> art history as a discipline saw a reaction against not only connoisseurship, and by extension the whole question of making attributions based on visual evidence, but against the study of artworks in their own right. In essence, the study of the object, be it a painting or a sculpture, became less important than the study of its context ... As a result, both art history and history as disciplines increasingly focused on identifying other elements that determined historical and art-historical 'outcomes', be they economic, social, or gender-based, in a headlong quest for generalization.

Reference has already been made to Desmond as a connoisseur, something he became only by training his inherently sound eye through repeated examination of houses, pictures, furniture and other man-made objects. The process started long before the current vogue for disparaging connoisseurship got underway: when Desmond was a young man, intuition based on experience was still highly regarded. He seems to have understood this, and to have realized the best means of refining his judgment was by looking and learning. Ultimately, the development of his connoisseurship was to benefit Ireland as much as it did him.

Desmond's aesthetic education began early, as did his lifelong passion for collecting. In 1988 he wrote how at the age of twelve, after seeing photographs of a statue of Hercules in front of a near-ruinous Ballynaguarde House in County Limerick, 'I was tempted to visit the place to see if any other statuary were left. Lying in a field a headless Andromeda chained to her rock was discovered near a clump of nettles, bought for £1 and triumphantly brought back to Glin. Her curvaceous marble form now decorates the summer house in the walled garden.' The statue remains at Glin still, installed in a rustic temple, its style inspired by astronomer and landscape designer Thomas Wright who came to Ireland in the 1740s and whose work for Irish patrons was discussed by Desmond in *Lost Demesnes*.

At an age when other boys would most likely be collecting stamps, Desmond had already turned his attention to other, potentially more valuable items. But if the value was to be realized he had to recognize it before anyone else. An undated letter to his mother from Stowe reports, 'I have bought £3.10.0 worth of crowns … If you sold them again you would get at least £6 for them so I think it was a good thing. They are lovely.' Another letter from around the same period advised:

> I have bought 3 crowns, one of Charles II, another of William III and another of George IV. They cost 10/= each but are worth 25/= each, and another two so I have got some bargains. There are some other ones also only I had not enough money but as they are worth double or treble what I bought them for I wonder would you send me some money for them, do tell me if you think it is a waste of money but I don't and I am now taking up coin collecting in serious so if you ever come across any you might try and get them.

The schoolboy Desmond had already begun to visit antique dealers; he first met lifelong friend John Harris in the mid 1950s when the latter was working in Geoffrey Houghton Brown's shop in London. As he grew older and his eye improved, so too grew the notion that Desmond might make a career in fine art. 'After my degree,' he wrote in August 1959 from Bali, 'there are various things I could do like working in a foundation, museum, etc. I suppose things sound unlucrative but even the business of dealing attracts me a good deal. I feel financially I could be very successful in this field. I could be a good salesman and buyer.' Gaining practice for this, while in Asia he bought jade and antiquities such as a bronze Buddha for his mother and stepfather and his letters of the time are full of information about what he had found and how much it had cost, usually after extensive negotiation.

During this period Desmond's interests were not yet primarily focused on Irish material. An undated letter sent from Leixlip Castle and therefore presumably dating from the early 1960s advises his mother:

> You know I bought the Venetian chair, green and gold XVIIIth century, quite beautiful, and the French Louis XV armchair, beechwood, old damask, good quality, and the mirror with cartouches, etc. These came to £300, very reasonable. Well, the dealer rang me up yesterday and needed money, so for an additional £450 he let me have 2 Chinese Chippendale chairs and the most scrummy desk & mirror that I have ever seen, probably by William Kent. Also an XVIIIth century marble statue of Rubens signed and dated 1756 by a very interesting Irish sculptor, pupil of Nollekens. I had to pay him then and there as he needed cash. I had wanted the chair & the desk for ages but before the desk was £600 and the chairs £100 each so I got them for £50 each and the desk for £300. These really are bargain prices for furniture of the *best* quality.

Another letter returns to the subject of these purchases, Desmond informing his mother that the desk

> is identical to plate CVIII in the 3rd edition of the Directory by Chippendale. If you have the reprint published by *Connoisseur* you can see it. Evidently it is highly likely that the piece is made in Chippendale's shop. Although Chippendale is out of fashion at the moment it is worth £1,000 according to my friend Tony Coleridge of Christie's. So I think £750 for all those pieces was a good buy.

Among the items mentioned above, the white marble statuette (of Van Dyck, not Rubens) was by Irish sculptor Geoghegan after one of a celebrated original pair by Michael Rysbrack; it had won a premium for Geoghegan from the Dublin Society in 1756. In the early 1960s Desmond paid £50 for this; in the Glin sale of May 2009 it sold for £32,450.

There appears to have been little further buying activity during Desmond's time at Harvard, presumably because he was absorbed in researching his thesis and teaching. On the other hand, the connections he made at the time, and the American collections both private and public that he had an opportunity to explore, stood to him many years later when he worked with James Peill on their book about Irish furniture. Some of the results of his Harvard years were manifest much earlier; in March 1967, for example, *Apollo* published an article by Desmond about the collection of New York publicist Benjamin Sonnenberg on display in the latter's Gramercy Park townhouse. Already Desmond was able to pick out items of specific interest to him, writing that Sonnenberg 'has an evident liking for Irish hunting-tables; no fewer than five are in the house, and with their generous oval-folded line and faded colour, they reflect the oval ceiling motifs so frequently found in Irish Adam-period plaster-work.'

Later in the same piece, he remarks that

> those interested in Irish furniture will be intrigued by a typical little mahogany tea-table, complete with scallop shell and Irish hock over the paw feet. Another Irish feature is the cross-hatching on the corners of the cabriole legs. It is just the sort of table from which Mrs Delaney might have dispensed tea at her villa, Delville, near Dublin, in the 1740s.

Here is Desmond the connoisseur, observing the distinctive characteristics of the eighteenth-century Irish furniture he loved and linking it to notable individuals of the same period.

After taking up his position at the V & A, Desmond had more money to collect items that caught his eye. From the late 1960s onwards, he started to collect documentation about Irish furniture and to acquire pieces for himself. Writing in *Apollo* in September 2005, he observed that 'It was possible to find Irish things in London cheaply then, as few knew anything about Irish furniture, and Irish collectors concentrated on silver and glass.' Almost no research had been undertaken on the specific characteristics of Irish furniture, which – as with the country's architecture and painting – was judged to be a provincial example of more refined English taste. Tellingly, when Desmond first wrote about the subject – in a piece co-authored by Anthony Coleridge whose monograph on Thomas Chippendale came out in

1968 – the article was entitled 'Eighteenth Century Irish Furniture: A Provincial Manifestation'. This appeared in the October 1966 issue of *Apollo* and opened by noting just how little had been hitherto written about Irish furniture. 'It is important to try to isolate the idiosyncratic differences between the mature English and the emergent Irish styles,' wrote the two authors. 'These distinguish the type of furniture which has unfortunately been gathered together under the misnomer "Irish Chippendale".'

The use of 'Irish Chippendale', coined by Constance Simon in her 1905 book *English Furniture Designers of the Eighteenth Century* and frequently employed by other specialists in the field thereafter, clearly irked Desmond, not least because it implied Irish Georgian furniture was indebted to that being produced in England. Typically, Owen Wheeler in 1907 had written: 'Summarised, this Erse work shows good material and carcase construction, but poor outline and inferior, lifeless carving.' Similarly, in 1921 the influential English furniture historian R.W. Symonds commented dismissively of Irish workmanship: 'The heavy appearance, superfluity of carved ornament, and absence of elegant and graceful lines that make its present-day appreciation and value considerably less than that of the contemporary English furniture.' In an important article on Irish furniture published by *Country Life* in February 1952, Symonds speculated why, to his mind, Irish furniture should be inferior to that produced in England and reached the conclusion: 'The answer is, I think, in the subtle influence of the land and its people. London was far away and the spirit of Ireland was at work.' That spirit, it is apparent, was considered not to benefit good design or production.

In trying to win support for Irish furniture, Desmond had to battle against entrenched prejudice. At least part of that prejudice can be explained by ignorance. The dispersal of house contents after 1900, and the failure to keep records of what these buildings once held, obviously provides part of the explanation for that ignorance, as do the losses connected with house burnings in the 1920s. As Desmond and James Peill wrote in their 2007 book on Irish furniture:

> The study of Irish houses can be difficult because so little documentation
> exists: in many cases either the bills or inventories survive for houses that
> have disappeared, or the houses where the furnishing have survived lack
> any documentation ... This lack of documentation, particularly accounts

and bills, has made it very difficult to identify craftsmen and it is rare indeed to find a house in Ireland with a muniment room storing such things as tradesmen's accounts which can be linked with the architecture, decoration and furnishing of the house itself.

Even within Ireland there was not much interest in the country's old furniture. As illustration of this domestic neglect, Desmond often told the story of a large table bought at auction in Dublin by Desmond Guinness. The latter was unable to see the piece properly because a row of bidders were sitting on top of it, but believing it to be a kitchen table, which is what was needed at Leixlip Castle, he bought the item for £3 10s. Only afterwards did he discover it was actually a richly carved mahogany sideboard of c.1750 that had come from Ballynaguarde, County Limerick – the same house where Desmond had paid £1 for the headless sculpture of Andromeda in the late 1940s.

In his article for *Apollo* in September 2005, Desmond explained that the piece had most likely been made for Edward Croker, who lived at Ballynaguarde and was a member of the notorious Limerick Hellfire Club. He went on to describe the sideboard, at the centre of which 'is a carved vase full of flowers flanked by great seaweedy festoons of fruit, flowers and foliage. Tiny lion masks peep out below shells and the heads on the legs look like Green Men tied on by rope.' This elaborate style of decoration, Desmond noted, was out of favour when the sideboard was bought for Leixlip and 'did not become fashionable or popular until at least twenty years later. Most people thought of such pieces as mawkish and ugly.'

It was largely thanks to Desmond's advocacy that attitudes started to change. (As indication of this, the Ballynaguarde sideboard was sold privately some ten years ago for a six-figure sum.) But that outcome could not have been predicted during much of the last century, a period when lack of interest in Irish furniture at home meant rich pickings for dealers overseas. In the 2007 book, Desmond and James Peill cited Thomas Rohan's *Confessions of a Dealer*, published in 1924, in which the author recalls Polish Jews travelling across Ireland 'selling cheap jewellery in order to get a foot through the door of these houses'. In 1913, the London dealer Burgess Hill of Maddox Street found it advantageous to advertise in *Connoisseur* magazine: 'From a variety of contributory causes, chiefly owing to the various Land Acts, the large landowners in Ireland have, during the past decade or so, been disposing of their land to the tenants, and consequently many lovely collections have been brought onto the market.'

The number of such disposals only increased as the century progressed, and since few in Ireland had either the income or inclination to buy, and there was no legislation to impede its departure, an enormous quantity of Irish furniture left the country. In a fascinating essay included in the catalogue accompanying their 2007 exhibition of Irish furniture (Desmond also contributed an essay to the same publication), Dublin antique dealers Chris and Paul Johnston describe how their father, who operated from premises on South William Street, exported enormous quantities of Irish-made pieces to the United States from the mid 1950s on. The two partners of a Manhattan antiques shop called Gramercy Galleries, for example, having bought from Paul Johnston senior on a number of occasions,

> told him to fill 40 ft containers as quickly as he could and ship them to New York. Beverly Smith of Harmony Row and South Anne Street facilitated this operation by paying for the furniture on behalf of Gramercy Galleries. As soon as the furniture arrived at Harmony Row to be packed the invoice was issued and paid. Often a load of furniture would arrive outside the shop, Dad would leave it on the truck, just label and number the piece, issue an invoice and send it off to Beverly Smith.

In the same essay, the Johnston brothers also recall the many English dealers such as Stuart Pattemore of Somerset who likewise saw opportunities in Ireland's indifference to its own heritage:

> Pattemore was a major shipper of furniture to the southern states of America and would come to Dublin and fill a pantechnicon of furniture every month, most of which would end up there. Thus, fine Irish, and indeed fine English furniture (which was here in abundance) came to leave Ireland in enormous quantities during the 1950s, 60s and early 70s.

The number of Irish country-house auctions escalated especially during the 1950s, but surviving catalogues demonstrate just how meagre was the information available to potential bidders; it took the expert eye of a dealer to see the value of a suite of furniture mixed up in a jumble of other lots. Writing in the 1992 IGS *Bulletin* about the dispersal of country-house contents, the late Cynthia O'Connor noted that on such occasions, 'Side by side with the domestic miscellany, the champagne glasses, the hip baths, were objects of first importance, which were on occasion overlooked and drifted away unrecognised, some to reappear at a later date in the foremost public galleries and museums of the world.'

O'Connor gave several examples of important items being lost to Ireland, such as the set of five mahogany chairs that were sold for £19 at the 12th Earl of Westmeath's sale at Pallas, County Galway, in 1934. When they reappeared forty years later at Sotheby Parke Bernet, New York, they fetched $207,500. 'By the time of the second spate of selling up, in and around the 1950s,' she wrote, 'English dealers and leading specialists in many fields were attending all the major auctions, their appetite whetted by romantic stories of the variety of unexpected finds in unexpected places and, dare one say, the ignorance of the natives.'

It was precisely this ignorance that Desmond set out to correct, determined that the high quality of Irish furniture be understood both in its country of origin and overseas. 'It's marvellous if you strike a rich field in its early days,' comments his former V&A colleague Ronald Lightbown, who remembers that at the time there was a strict rule whereby members of museum staff were not permitted to buy anything the institution might want to acquire without first bringing it to the relevant authority's notice. If there was no interest, then a private purchase could be made. 'Desmond went around all the dealers,' says Lightbown. 'He'd roam out each lunchtime and if he saw objects of interest to your department, he'd bring them to your attention.'

Naturally, there was no interest in the V&A in Irish furniture, so Desmond was able to buy as much as he could afford. Among the pieces he picked up in those days was a rare George II giltwood mirror made around 1750 by Dublin brothers John and Francis Booker and, exceptionally, carrying the remains of their label on its reverse ('Then I lost the label,' Desmond told me in 2009. 'I found it again in a box of rubbish in the office.') The mirror was discovered at Phillips & Harris of Kensington Church Street in 1970 (and its acquisition provided the basis for an article by Desmond on the Booker family published by *Country Life* in January 1971); Desmond bought it, together with a little Irish mahogany tea table, for less than £600.

A few years later, from a shop on the Fulham Road he bought an equally important piece of Irish furniture, a George II mahogany bureau writing cabinet, again dating from the mid eighteenth century. Desmond told me in May 2007: 'It wasn't that expensive: it must have been around £800 or £1000, simply inconceivable today.' Inconceivable indeed: two years after that comment the writing cabinet sold in the 2009 Glin sale for £91,250 (and the Booker mirror went for £51,650).

The catalogue for the sale makes for instructive reading, not least because it demonstrates how much had changed since Desmond began to collect Irish furniture, and how – thanks to his own research – much more is now known about Irish furniture. The majority of lots offered at Christie's had been acquired by him since the mid 1960s, as and when finances permitted. A fine Irish George II mahogany side table, its apron centred on a scallop shell, was bought from Dublin dealer Gerald Kenyon in the early 1970s, while a pair of Irish George II side chairs were acquired around the same time from David Drey on the King's Road in London. Desmond's old friend Christopher Gibbs was the source for several fine pieces, such as a superlative carved George II mahogany side table bearing the arms of the Creagh family of County Cork, and another George II mahogany side table with a marble top.

Eventually, these pieces found their way to Glin but at least some of them, when first acquired, were installed in Desmond's London flat on Pont Street, gradually displacing other items as his taste refined. A feature on the flat published in *Vogue* during this period gives an insight into how he lived at the time and how diverse as yet were his collecting habits (the article describes him as having 'specialised interests in the history of ornament and Italian baroque pictures'). A series of interconnected rooms, the space was filled with furnishings from different periods and countries; in the living room close by a Viennese Biedermeier-period cylinder desk hung a painting by the eighteenth-century Roman artist Pier Leone Ghezzi, while the dining room contained a rococo silver ewer on a maplewood table, the floor covered by an art nouveau needlework carpet. The walls of each room were painted in bold colours, a reflection of Mariga Guinness' influence.

'Desmond FitzGerald is a passionately knowledgeable collector,' observes the accompanying text,

> who backs his fancy to the limit, often buying unsigned paintings and drawings in improbable places solely because they give him visual pleasure.

Needless to say, his scholarly and catholic interests impel him to seek the provenance of any work of art he buys. 'I buy them solely because I like them. So many collectors are suckers for labels and the reassurance of art critics and dealers. Attributions can sometimes take years, but the quest is fascinating ...'

The same article also reported that Desmond claimed his flat was among the cheapest of its kind in London, 'thanks to no heating and minimal conveniences. Such deficiencies are readily countered by any Irishman ...' Desmond's old friend, decorator David Mlinaric, helped to set up the Pont Street residence and remembers that 'he didn't have a kitchen for the first year or so; there was an old stove standing next to a sink. I remember the day before his first wedding Loulou's mother Maxime and her brother Alexis going to buy a kitchen, it was Maxime's present to the couple.' On the other hand, Mlinaric regards Desmond's taste in the arrangement of his reception rooms as unerring:

> There wasn't much I could do he wouldn't have been able to do himself. Desmond shopped, I mixed the colours and did a bit of upholstery, the furniture was all his taste. Taste: it's in the DNA. You either have it or you don't. In the world of art historians, of that whole group I can think of only two that could do the practical, and did so for themselves. One was Gervase Jackson-Stops, the other Desmond.

The same point was made by John Cornforth writing in *Country Life* in June 1998, when he commented that Desmond possessed a rare talent: 'as well as having a keen eye for objects, he has one for arrangement and decoration'.

Desmond's taste, according to Eddie McParland, 'was instant and impeccable. I can only decide what colour my walls should be after weeks of humming and hawing but he was always decisive. Glin is a testament to how he knew how to do things.' 'His taste was classical, really,' says decorator John Stefanidis, who also saw a lot of Desmond during the London years. 'He didn't really like anything contemporary but he did have a very good eye and so could judge if something was good or bogus. I remember once getting a chair on approval and asking his opinion: he was furious and kicked it!' Stefanidis notes how, for Desmond, 'it always had to do with Ireland, you see. One of the reasons he would like a picture or piece of furniture, for example, was because it was Irish and he wanted to save it.' Another old friend, former editor of *The World of Interiors*, Min Hogg, observes of Desmond's taste: 'The limitations were that he was so obsessed with everything Irish – he was utterly and completely Irish – and that was the nub of it.'

Hogg also makes the point that throughout his life Desmond was a passionate collector: 'He couldn't stop shopping, like a mad acquisitive aunt.' Speaking to *Saga* magazine in October 2000, Desmond rhetorically asked, 'How can you ever say any collection is complete? There will never come a time when I can rest.' In May 2007, shortly before his book on Irish furniture was published, I spoke to Desmond about his approach to decorating, which he summarized as 'I suppose controlled clutter really' before going on to call his acquisitiveness 'obsessional' and commenting, 'I'm always looking, always buying. Once a collector, you know.'

At the time, I noted two characteristics of Desmond's sensibility: the manner in which it had focused more and more on Ireland, and its development within the tightest of budgets. Biding his time, waiting for the right moment, the right piece, the right price: these had come to be the distinguishing characteristics of Desmond's collecting career. It took a lot of time and trouble to find the items he wanted, he explained to me, pondering why more people weren't prepared to wait. 'Looking at modern interiors,' he said, 'I don't understand why only one little picture is hung on a wall; to my mind, it looks rather insipid. Then there's this fashion for hanging mirrors in gold frames over the chimney ...' His voice, I remember, trailed away in palpable disappointment (Desmond often had difficulty accepting that other people did not share his interests or tastes).

Never a minimalist, nor did Desmond believe in clutter for its own sake. Each object in any of the rooms of his houses had been carefully selected for just that setting. Moreover, it had inherent aesthetic merit independent of its place in the greater whole. 'There's a difference between being an academic and being interested in display,' comments David Mlinaric. 'Mariga was a great fan of artifice and display, whereas Desmond was a connoisseur.'

Writing of Glin Castle in *Country Life* in June 1998, John Cornforth remarked:

> It is an unusual collector's house because it does not feel like one: every-
> thing looks as though it has always been there, and the recent arrivals

are completely at ease with the ancestors. So, without the Knight as guide, no one could guess how everything has come together. Although he will explain how he has brought items back to Ireland from Australia or British Columbia, it takes more digging to discover how and why they relate to his researches into Irish fine and applied arts and to his own romantic patriotism.

In these few lines Cornforth draws attention to several aspects of Desmond as connoisseur, not least his ability to blend recently acquired pieces with those already in his possession.

Moreover, as Cornforth pointed out, whether old or new, every item not only reflected Desmond's impeccable eye but also his never-ending investigation into the history of Ireland's fine and decorative arts. From the era of the Pont Street flat onwards, his homes were evolving museums; laboratories of research in which Irish craftsmanship was simultaneously analysed and celebrated. It was also presented in a particularly alluring manner, again a tribute to Desmond's unerring judgment, matched by that of his second wife Olda. 'Decoration on its own can create dead houses,' observed Cornforth,

> with objects that often play only a role of pattern-making, but at Glin everything has a reason for being there. That applies not only to the principal portraits and pieces of furniture but extends to every watercolour of an Irish country house, the Irish topographical prints and engraved portraits, the maps and caricatures and even cut paper-work … These objects build up into considered groups that flow through corridors, up stairs and into bedrooms and bathrooms.

I emphasize Desmond's personal taste and his evolution as a collector because of the impact these had on him as a scholar. This, in turn, had repercussions throughout Ireland. Academics can spend a lifetime immersed in their chosen area of research without ever engaging with the subject emotionally: thought and feeling remain unconnected. This was most certainly not true of Desmond, and it helps to explain why he abandoned his thesis and academia. He felt too much and too passionately to be a detached scholar. Instead, three powerful character traits led to his becoming a connoisseur: love of Ireland, love of history and love of beauty. Combined with a naturally quizzical intellect, Desmond inevitably made himself the pre-eminent expert on the visual and decorative arts in Ireland. As with Irish painting and archi-tecture, he wanted to know more about Irish furniture because it meant something to him personally, because his response to these objects was visceral and intense and persistent. Having discovered the sterling qualities of Irish craftsmanship, he deter-mined to bring them to the attention of anyone who might be interested. Hence his lifelong preparedness not just to write and publish on the subject, but to share material he had uncovered, another trait rarely encountered in academic circles. Desmond was by instinct an evangelist but he understood that in order to gain converts to the cause he would first need to marshal sound arguments. This, as much as his own inherent curiosity, was why he undertook so much diligent research.

What remains astounding is not just Desmond's stamina in undertaking that research but also the length of time he often spent collecting snippets and scraps of material in the expectation they would eventually find a purpose. This was certainly the case with his investigation into Irish Georgian furniture. Following the publica-tion of the article on this subject co-written with Anthony Coleridge and published by *Apollo* in October 1966, Desmond continued to find out what he could. He was aided by his work at the V&A, since it allowed him to compare Irish pieces with those within the institution's collection and to begin defining the characteristics of Irish-made furniture. During these years he wrote extensively about English craftsmanship, beginning in January 1966 with an essay on the rococo music room from Norfolk House, London, which appeared in the V&A's *Bulletin* and was later expanded into a small book (the Norfolk House room had been installed in the museum since 1938).

Other similar articles followed over the next few years, among them 'Chip-pendale's place in the English Rococo' (*Journal of the Furniture History Society*, vol. 4, 1968), 'The mural from 44 Grosvenor Square' (*Victoria and Albert Museum Year Book*, 1969) and 'Gravelot and his influence on English furniture' (*Apollo*, August, 1969). These pieces should be mentioned because they show that when Desmond came to focus almost exclusively on Irish Georgian furniture, which he did after moving back to Ireland in the mid 1970s, he brought with him an understanding of the wider world of which it was part.

As has been mentioned, Desmond had long since become an inveterate haunter of antique shops and this activity, conducted at lunchtimes and over weekends, immeasurably improved his knowledge. In the introduction to the 2007 book on Irish furniture, Desmond explained how in the late 1960s he had started building up a collection of photographs of Irish furniture with a view to producing just such a work. An archive gradually took shape and eventually grew to more than 2000 images, all filed at Glin. This archive, generously donated in 2009 to NUI Maynooth and now stored at Castletown, County Kildare, demonstrates how Desmond never ceased to work; never missed an opportunity to gather additional information. So as well as an abundance of clippings from newspapers, magazines and auction catalogues, there are hundreds of photographs of pieces of furniture that Desmond had seen. These pictures are rarely of high quality – and sometimes appear to have been taken at a drinks party or dinner – but this scarcely mattered since they were not intended for publication, merely to serve as an aide-memoire. Carrying details of location and date, they were added to the stock of other material to create a unique resource on which he would be able to draw when the time was right.

Once it became known that he had that resource, he was often asked for advice on pieces of furniture that owners thought might be Irish in origin. Typical in this respect is a letter he wrote to a couple in New Orleans in April 1996 about a mirror in their possession: Desmond was able to send them a copy of a sales report he had kept from a Christie's auction almost twenty years earlier. Diligently gathering large amounts of documentation over decades, he was certain that eventually it all would serve a purpose. 'It quickly became apparent,' he wrote in 2007, 'that if any real and useful judgement was to be made about Irish furniture, as many different examples as possible needed to be gathered together, collated and compared. Likewise, years of research lay ahead combined with my work for books on other Irish fields: architecture, landscape gardening and painting.'

One other area of assistance Desmond does not mention here is his work as Christie's representative in Ireland from the mid 1970s. Before discussing the beneficial consequences of this association, it would be as well to consider the criticism Desmond attracted because of his job. Nicknamed 'The Knight of Odd Lots' by satirical magazine *Phoenix*, he was judged hypocritical in some quarters for championing the cause of conservation and promoting the merits of Irish decorative arts while simultaneously engaging in the sale of Irish work through an English auction house. As his former Christie's colleague Ted Clive wrote after Desmond's death,

'He embodied the contradiction that exists within many of us: a passionate interest in the preservation of historic collections and the need to source the very best property for sale.'

A profile of Desmond carried by *Phoenix* in October 1983 ironically described him as being 'caught on the horns of a truly terrible dilemma' before posing the question:

> When in the course of his worthy researches into Irish antiquities he comes across undiscovered gems of Irish heritage, what should he do? Should he move mountains to ensure they remain in Ireland or should he activate the telex to Christie's in London and get his own scavengers on the job before that nasty lot from Sotheby's get wind of the loot?

Of course, Desmond was perfectly aware of the ambiguity inherent in his association with Christie's. 'I've been a conflict of interests all my life,' he told the *Sunday Independent*'s Victoria Mary Clarke in November 2002. 'But I know where my motivation lies which is to get as much stuff as possible brought back here.' In that last sentence lies the best answer that can be given to his critics: that by raising the profile of their furniture, painting and fine art, Desmond hoped the Irish people would come to appreciate it better and ensure its retention in the country.

'In Desmond's case the collection at stake was an entire nation's artistic patrimony,' wrote Ted Clive in his tribute, 'and he spent much of his life fighting to preserve as much as possible of what had been created and collected in Ireland during the British ascendancy. Until quite recently he did this in the face of the opposition or indifference of the Irish government.' For decades, works of art had left Ireland in large quantities because no legislation existed to impede their removal. Furthermore, anyone buying Irish art outside of the country had to pay a high level of VAT when bringing it back to Ireland. Far from encouraging the preservation of cultural heritage, the Irish state was assisting its dispersal to foreign buyers. This absurd and invidious situation was highlighted in July 1983 when Desmond Guinness sold a group of Irish paintings in London through Christie's. Among those attending the auction was then director of the National Gallery of Ireland Homan Potterton, who unsuccessfully tried to buy some of the pictures for his institution. Afterwards he told *The Irish Times*' Maeve Binchy:

If an Irish buyer paid £60,000 sterling for a picture, at today's rate he would have to pay almost £80,000 in Irish punts. Then there is a really crippling VAT which would have to be paid of 23 per cent at point of entry. It's certainly no inducement to an Irish collector, and no help to an Irish gallery, is it?

On the same occasion, Desmond answered the charge that because of his job he was in part responsible for the depletion of Ireland's artistic heritage. 'I do get a lot of attacks,' he replied, 'and people have said I am a hypocrite, but quite honestly I feel that I have my own integrity. I am in the business of buying pictures for people as well as selling them, and I could buy a great many more pictures for Ireland and Irish people if these extraordinary difficulties were not put in our way.' Responding to similar accusations of humbug because of his job, Desmond told Hugh Montgomery-Massingberd (*Town & Country*, October 1993):

> For a start, it is surely of considerable benefit to have someone doing the Christie's job who knows and cares passionately for the subject. I do all in my power to see if the pieces being offered for sale can possibly stay in or return to Ireland. It may seem a paradox, but I have spoken out strongly of the need for a new licensing system to *control* the export of works of art from Ireland.

Particularly in circumstances where so little assistance was provided for the maintenance of historic houses and their contents, there was nothing Desmond could do to stop owners of Irish artworks placing these on the market: if somebody needed to dispose of furniture or paintings, an auction house – whether Christie's or another – was almost certainly going to be involved. With or without Desmond, the sale would perforce take place because there were no mechanisms within Ireland to help impoverished proprietors hold on to their inherited possessions, or to keep those possessions in the country. This was especially the case during the 1970s and 1980s when the Irish state nonchalantly watched a series of great houses dispose of their contents, beginning with the Malahide Castle sale in May 1976 and continuing through to that at Luttrellstown Castle in September 1983. Christie's was involved in the majority of these occasions and, as Ted Clive observes, 'Our success was frequently attributable to Desmond's legendary persuasive charm.' During those years he most often worked with two other Christie's staff, his old friend Tony

Coleridge and Charles Hindlip. The latter afterwards remembered, 'Desmond was very clever and full of wonderful contradictions as well as oysters. Tony and I had more fun with Desmond at those Irish sales than anything else we ever did; and we always turned in a profit.' Just because he did his job well, it should not be assumed Desmond necessarily enjoyed the task. 'I was like a funeral director at many important Irish sales,' he remembered when speaking to *The New York Times*' Wendy Moonan in April 2007. 'In those days Ireland's grand houses were being dismantled.'

Furthermore, despite his position with Christie's Desmond constantly spoke of the need for the Irish government to introduce controls over the export of art from the country. 'In Ireland we've lost so much,' he told *The Irish Times*' Elgy Gillespie in January 1980. 'Not that I think one place should have everything, we needn't be parochial about art, which is ultimately international. But we do have more cause to be worried about the drift of paintings and antiques than other countries.' One obvious problem arising from this drift was that it went almost totally unchronicled. The big country-house auctions might have received a certain amount of attention, but many other properties gradually lost their contents as these were quietly sold by owners who needed to pay for a new roof or improved heating. Without an official record of any kind being kept, items of national importance simply left the country, their departure unrecorded, their absence unremarked. Thereby Ireland's cultural patrimony had steadily and insidiously diminished. It was a situation that rightly infuriated Desmond who, in the same 1980 interview, proposed the government should create 'a viewing committee which would at least record and photograph the things if not stop them from going ...'

For much of his lifetime no institution like the National Gallery of Ireland or the National Museum of Ireland was even consulted before paintings or furniture were taken out of the country to be offered for sale in another jurisdiction. On the other hand, as has been pointed out, buyers wishing to repatriate Irish artwork were faced with a punitive tax for doing so.

Far from being disadvantageous to Ireland, there were a number of benefits to Desmond being employed by Christie's. In the first place, he persuaded the company to help fund a number of projects close to his heart, such as the preservation of Castletown, County Kildare (a valuation day held there by Christie's in 1983, for example, raised £2000 for the Castletown Foundation), and the publication of

Vanishing Country Houses of Ireland. In addition, Desmond's unparalleled knowledge of Irish houses and fine art meant that he was able to recognize the value of works that would otherwise have gone unremarked. This was true not just within Ireland but also around the world: thanks to his scholarship, Desmond often spotted Irish items in other countries and ensured they were duly listed with the correct country of origin. He would then seek to secure their return to Ireland, either to one of the state institutions or to a private buyer. He was always passionate that Irish works of art find a home in Ireland and worked hard to see this happen. His impressive range of contacts among collectors allowed him to advise them of what to buy in sales. Desmond especially encouraged Irish buyers, bringing suitable lots to their attention, guiding them towards making the best purchases. As a result, there are today a number of outstanding collections of furniture and fine art in Ireland for the existence of which he deserves a generous measure of the credit.

There may be readers who regard the above arguments as specious but frankly the only alternative to Desmond's efforts was that Ireland would continue to haemorrhage her cultural heritage. Speaking to Walter Ellis of *The Sunday Telegraph* in April 1989, he bemoaned the current state of affairs: 'Here, our heritage is being eroded. It's not just the loss of paintings. It's furniture. It's buildings. The whole structure of our cultural background is being neglected. It's simply not being looked after – and yet the heritage is a large part of what people come to Ireland *for*.' By persistently drawing attention to the quality and value of the country's fine and decorative arts, by writing and speaking on the same subject, by discovering lost items and attempting to bring them back to Ireland, Desmond did far more for Irish art and for helping to keep as much of it as possible in Ireland than had his armchair critics.

Ironically, bringing the pecuniary value of Irish furniture to public attention worked to Desmond's disadvantage. Even as he tried to keep pieces in Ireland, rising prices made them more attractive for foreign buyers. 'A good side table used to cost a few hundred,' he told *The Times*' Tim Willis in September 1990. 'Now it will go to America for £30,000 to £40,000.' In 2007, he explained to me that over previous decades, when finances permitted, he had

> refurnished Glin with Irish pieces and Irish paintings. I was lucky to have
> been able to prowl around the London antique shops after I took up a

curatorship at the Victoria and Albert Museum in 1965 ... It was possible to find Irish things in London cheaply then, as few knew anything about Irish furniture, and Irish collectors concentrated on silver and glass.

But the more notice he drew to such items, the higher the prices they realized and the less he was able to afford them.

By the end of the century, the option of picking up Irish furniture cheaply no longer existed. Writing in *Art at Auction* in March 1999, Clinton R. Howell observed: 'Irish furniture has become very popular in the last few years with the economic resurgence of Ireland – and those prescient collectors who did not mind the offbeat nature of what they were buying, have benefitted from this recovery.' Desmond had been one of those prescient collectors but increasingly found it hard to afford the prices being sought. 'When I first started to collect,' he told Sue Blackhall of *Saga* in August 2000, 'there was no interest in Irish antiques. Then no-one valued them at all. But pieces are now increasingly beyond my means.' An illustration of this change in attitudes, and consequent increase in price, is provided by the sale at Christie's in November 2005 of an Irish George II mahogany pier glass attributed to John Houghton and dating from *c.* 1740. Expected to make in the region of £30,000–£50,000, in fact the lot went for £192,800.

In August 1998, Desmond wrote an introduction to the handsome catalogue produced by antique dealers Chris and Paul Johnston to coincide with an exhibition of Irish Georgian furniture they presented in Newman House, Dublin. Where once their father had exported containerloads of such work from the country, they were responsible for returning at least some of it to Ireland. 'It is somewhat of an occasion,' Desmond commented,

> to see the gathering together of a collection of Irish 18th century furniture in Dublin. This reverses the trend of the past 80 years or so which saw the exportation of so much Irish art and decorative arts to England, the United States and elsewhere. It is therefore a comment on changing economic times when we see a now prosperous Ireland attracting back to its shores part of its artistic heritage.

Desmond could claim a fair measure of the credit for attracting back Ireland's artistic heritage, even if he was no longer able to afford the prices it now made.

Whatever about the drawbacks of the job from his perspective, as far as Christie's was concerned Desmond proved to be an ideal presence in Ireland. Nicholas White, who joined the firm in 1993 and is now a senior director, remembers: 'From the point of view of trying to put sales together, Desmond was absolutely ideal. He knew everyone, they all knew who he was, he had a profile. It simply wouldn't have been possible to do Irish sales without him.' What White describes as Desmond's 'obsessiveness about houses and families' was also invaluable to Christie's:

> When we were putting together catalogues invariably there'd be some last-minute worry. I'd ring up Desmond at the final proofing stage, he'd go away and then the fax would start whirring and all the links to houses and families you could ever have would come through. How many people could do that? Have all the information on Irish families and furniture and pictures and houses, and how they all relate?

Desmond's unique ability to provide such connections remained an invaluable resource even after he had formally retired from his position with the company in 2000.

'He never really did go,' says another Christie's senior director Ted Clive. 'When he was in London he always popped in, and he retained the ability to twist everyone around his finger. He was frightfully good at getting you to do things, it was the way he asked, he was always very, very effective.'

Finally, it must be acknowledged that the link with Christie's was beneficial to Desmond's research into various areas of Irish art. Already familiar with many houses in Ireland, he now had a job that gave him a reason to visit still more. In the course of work-related journeys about the country – in 1980 he estimated this involved driving some 40,000 miles per annum – Desmond discovered houses and their contents that had previously been unknown to him. The importance of those contents was just as often unknown to their owners. Even if they were not interested in selling, it was helpful for them to be better informed about what was in their possession. And it was equally helpful for Desmond to know what items of furniture and fine art remained in Ireland, and to have an opportunity to study these.

Christies brush with Irish

SEARCH FOR PAINTINGS . . . Desmond FitzGerald, Irish representative with Christies prepares for the forthcoming sale in Dublin

A WORLD class auction house have begun their door to door search for top Irish paintings.

Consultants from Christies will be scouring Dublin's attics and walls over the next few months to find valuable paintings by Ireland's established and unknown artists.

And it could prove a real "windfall" for many families, as a painting by an unknown artist fetched £85,000 in a similar search several years ago.

"Unfortunately there are a lot of fakes around in Ireland at the moment and this brings some artist's prices down," said Desmond Fitz-Gerald, Christies representative in Ireland.

He explained that any paintings discovered would be put into a December sale at Dublin's Royal Hiberian Academy and that Christies take a ten per cent commission on the price fetched.

"If you believe you have a valuable painting then the best thing to do is send me a snap of it. I can pretty much tell from that what·it may be," said Desmond.

He added that most paintings they view are "junk", while some are "worthless" reproductions and prints. And he warned families who believe they may own a valuable painting to only deal with "reputable dealers or auctioneers".

Anyone who believes they have a valuable work of art on their hands can write to Desmond at Glin Castle, Glin, Co. Limerick.

Ever the tireless publicist, Desmond looking for lots for one of the first Irish art auctions held by Christie's in Dublin. Evening Herald, 5 September 1990.

He continued delving into whatever written sources could be found for infor-mation about the development and manufacture of Irish furniture and decorative goods from the late seventeenth century. No Irish cabinetmaker or furniture-manu-facturer archives exist and even identification labels and marks are rare. In order to trace the history of eighteenth-century Irish furniture the student needs to look for alternative sources of information. This is what Desmond did. As he wrote in his introduction to the catalogue produced for the Johnston brothers' 1998 exhibition of Irish Georgian furniture:

> A close study of Dublin 18th century newspapers shows how the furnishing trade grew. Advertisements proliferate as the century goes on and auction notices show the amount of elaborate suites of seat furniture, commodes, high and low boys, console tables, gilt mirrors, paintings and prints which comprised the contents and decorations of those splendid Dublin houses and Georgian mansions all over the countryside.

Long before anyone else, Desmond undertook that close study and some of the results of his inquiries were periodically published. He had already written general pieces on Irish furniture, such as a small book about the subject produced in 1978, and five years later a chapter covering the same ground in *Ireland: A Cultural Encyclopaedia*, edited by Brian de Breffny. As his research produced more informa-tion, so the work he published was able to be more specialized, as can be seen in such articles as 'Dublin directories and trade labels' (*Furniture History: The Journal of the Furniture History Society*, vol. 21, 1985), 'Early Irish trade-cards and other eighteenth-century ephemera' (*Eighteenth-Century Ireland*, vol. 2, 1987) and 'The marquetry decoration of early 18th century Irish Furniture' (*Irish Arts Review*, vol. 13, 1997).

Also worthy of mention are 'A Directory of the Dublin Furnishing Trade, 1752–1800', which appeared in *Decantations: A Tribute to Maurice Craig* (1992) and 'Russborough – its decoration and furniture, some preliminary thoughts' in Sergio Benedetti's 1997 exhibition catalogue for the National Gallery of Ireland, *The Milltowns, A Family Reunion*. Other scholars were also entering the field during this period and Desmond was happy to give due credit to their endeavours; in his 1998 essay for the Johnston brothers, he cited the work of Susan Foster and Toby Barnard, mentioning the latter's 'painstaking trawling through estate papers, inventories and

Irish manuscript material' in order to throw clearer light on the manufacture and consumption of furniture and fine art in Georgian Ireland.

John Rogers is another who engaged in similarly assiduous research as a result of Desmond's urging. 'One of the things he was really good at was suggesting new ideas to people. Because he was a polymath, he got the ball rolling for lots of other people. I can't think of anyone in my generation who'd have his breadth of knowledge.' In John Rogers' case, Desmond proposed additional research into the subject of eighteenth-century Irish tradesmen's labels; this was in the late 1980s after he had published his own articles on the subject.

> At that point, there were a lot of names but not much linking of them, who was who, what was what; it was like one of those children's games of Join the Dots. So I went through about fifty years of *Faulkner's Dublin Journal* looking for references to luxury tradesmen or woodworkers, and then I handed all that in to him.

Thanks to specialist research of this sort being encouraged by Desmond, interest in the subject grew further and in 2000, two years after their first exhibition of Irish Georgian furniture, the Johnston brothers presented a second such event, this time in Dublin's Merrion Hotel. Desmond was invited to write an introduction to the accompanying catalogue, in cognisance of his pivotal role in this area. He took the opportunity to note how, even in the short period since the last show, interest in the subject both in academic circles and in the salesroom had continued to increase. For example, Desmond's old employer, the Victoria and Albert Museum, had been the venue in February 1999 for the Furniture History Society's first symposium devoted to Irish furniture, with papers on such topics as eighteenth-century looking glasses and nineteenth-century cabinetmakers. These were subsequently published together with an introduction by Desmond in which he rejoiced that so much regard was finally being paid to this subject after such a long period of neglect, and listed many of the scholars undertaking work in the field. The following September the Irish Georgian Society repeated the occasion in collaboration with the National Museum of Ireland at Collins Barracks, Dublin.

The Furniture History Society followed up its own event with a tour of Ireland, North and South, in May 2000. A discipline previously of interest only to a handful of individuals like Desmond now attracted ever-growing numbers of buyers and scholars. 'Amazing salesroom prices have been achieved over the last year or so,' he wrote with an evident sense of wonder in his introduction to the Johnston brothers' second catalogue, 'and these prices concentrate the minds of collectors and dealers alike, and the popularity of the subject may mean that more scholarly attention follows. The extraordinary variety, both weird and wonderful, plain and elegant, of Irish furniture is now being fully appreciated and sought after.'

Ultimately, all of Desmond's research into Irish Georgian furniture led to the publication in 2007 of a ground-breaking book on the subject, co-authored with James Peill. It had been a long time in gestation. In the course of a conversation with John Richardson published in Andy Warhol's *Interview* magazine in 1978, Desmond remarked:

> I've just finished a small booklet on Irish furniture. Irish furniture is another very individual subject because just between the 1730s and the 1760s it had developed an animal style ... You get these extraordinary exaggerated masks and paw feet. You imagine this kind of furniture is going to walk or even dance around the floor. I hope to do a full length book on this subject in the near future.

At the time, he was in discussion about collaborating on just such a work with Andrew Phelan, an Irish-born circuit judge based in London who had also undertaken a great deal of research into Irish furniture. The two men wrote to each other extensively about the proposed book and mapped out what form it might take but in the end the proposal came to nothing. One reason for this is that Desmond's attention was focused on the book about Irish watercolours with Anne Crookshank and so, as he advised Andrew Phelan, he had little spare time for another project. Perhaps this was as well, since the amount of material that would then have been available was far less than would be the case even a couple of decades later.

In the event, almost thirty years were to pass before the book appeared, not least because Desmond had to wait until he did find the right person with whom to work on the project. He and James Peill first met when the latter, then still a university undergraduate, was working as an intern at Christie's. 'I was about to go on a camping tour around Ireland looking at ruins, and Desmond said you must come to see Glin when you're over, so I did.' In 1994, Peill joined Christie's as a graduate trainee and after a year entered the auction house's furniture department.

> Whenever a piece of Irish furniture came up, I'd show it to Desmond. It was he who proposed we collaborate together on a book. At the time, it was probably 1996, he was working with Anne Crookshank on *Irish Painters*. He had to finish that book, and after he had he said to me, why not come over to Glin and see the box files there. There was a Furniture Society trip to Ireland [May 2000] and it went to Glin. Desmond took me off to see all the material he had collected, and we decided to do it.

In the book's foreword, the Furniture History Society's president Nicholas Goodison remembered that it was when the organization had visited Glin that he

> encouraged James Peill to run with the Knight's vision to co-author a book on Irish furniture. There has long been a gaping hole on the shelves of furniture enthusiasts waiting to be filled by a history of Irish furniture and carving and the Knight of Glin's intention to write the definitive guide has been known for longer than his co-author has been alive.

There was a 34-year age difference between the two men, yet Desmond spotted the appropriate collaborator for a project that had long been close to his heart: a definitive account of Irish Georgian furniture. 'He'd been collecting Irish furniture, and photographs of it since before I was born,' says Peill who believes the reason Desmond invited him to work on the new book was because 'I had a strong interest in Irish arts and furniture and he didn't know anyone else who had the same interest.' Their collaborative process was almost identical to the working methods used by Desmond and Anne Crookshank. 'I could use a computer,' says Peill, remembering that Desmond would sometimes enquire of someone from whom they needed help, 'Do you think we should sent them an "*email*"?'

> I would type and he'd dictate. There'd be times when I'd lead the prose, and times he would but neither of us was so strong-willed to overwhelm the other. I had better technical knowledge of English and Irish furniture, he brought the broader picture and the context of Ireland. And he had an amazing collection of quotes that he'd been collecting as snippets for years for this book. He wasn't, unlike a lot of people in the

furniture-history world, interested only in furniture: he would go into a house and look at the entirety.

The collaboration seems to have been entirely happy – 'by the time I got to know him the volcano had died down' – and based on mutual respect. 'He liked the company and he liked the rapport,' says James Peill. 'Writing can be a lonely business. He loved being able to bounce ideas off someone else and to chat about it, because he was a gregarious person. And Desmond loved footnotes: one of the wonders of technology was that we could introduce them all the time.'

Those footnotes permitted Desmond to include additional pieces of information he had gathered over the preceding decades. James Peill tells a story, confirmed by Olda FitzGerald, of Desmond and Olda once staying with the present Marquess of Lansdowne at Bowood House, Wiltshire, where Desmond discovered a quote from an eighteenth-century Countess of Shelburne regarding Castletown, County Kildare. Desmond asked if he might make a copy, a request that was refused, but he went ahead anyway and was caught doing so. It was, says Olda tactfully, 'rather awkward' but also an indication of his determination to source every available scrap of material regarding Irish furniture history. 'The books at Glin really came into their own when we were writing there,' James Peill remembers. 'I'd be in front of the computer and Desmond would go scurrying off and find exactly the right book and the right quote. Olda always joked that whenever they went on holiday, they would come back with luggage twice the weight because of all the books Desmond bought.'

Irish Furniture, in turn, proved to be a substantial volume, not least thanks to the necessary abundance of photography by James Fennell and Dara McGrath. As for the text, it brought together more than forty years of Desmond's research combined with James Peill's more recent analysis, the result a work that was both informative and stimulating. As Simon Swynfen Jervis commented when reviewing the book for *The Burlington*:

> Clearly *Irish Furniture* establishes itself as at once a work of reference and the platform for future studies. But it is also a handsome production informed by an international perspective, by the absence of that *de bas en haut* feeling of resentment which sometimes affects studies of a culture strongly influenced by a more powerful neighbour, and by a certain genial zest.

Above: *The entrance hall of Glin Castle in the late 1950s, its decoration far less elaborate than it would become over the following decades as Desmond gradually built up an unrivalled collection of Irish furniture and art.*

Below: *The entrance hall of Glin Castle today, after Desmond's many additions all of which look as though they have been in place for centuries.*

Desmond and Loulou de la Falaise on board RMS Queen Mary *returning to Europe after their honeymoon in the United States.*

Christmas
1967
Florrie and
Jack Phillips
Mama & Ray
Alain de la Falaise
GLIN

Christmas 1967 at Glin Castle, where the house party included Desmond's mother and stepfather as well as an old friend from Harvard, Florence Phillips, and her husband Jack.

me (just thro')   Antonia Thynne   David Mlinaric   George Stacpoole

Louise   Christopher Sykes   Christopher Thynne   Valerie and Thomas Pakenham

Houseguests at Glin were invariably taken on expeditions to explore buildings in the area. Here on a visit to Dromore Castle are Desmond and Louise, Thomas and Valerie Pakenham, George Stacpoole, Christopher Sykes, Christopher and Antonia Thynne and David Mlinaric.

A photograph taken by their friend Christopher Thynne to mark the wedding in August 1970 of Desmond and Olda Willes.

At a party given by Olda's parents in London's Ritz Hotel in December 1970 to mark her marriage, Paddy Moloney plays the whistle while Desmond, Raymond O'Neill, Garech Browne and Nicholas Gormanston attempt to dance.

Maurice Craig, Mick Jagger, Robert Fraser, Paddy.

Mick & Maurice

Mick, Jenny, Olda.

Talitha Tony Bertie

A weekend house party at Glin in 1970 where the diverse guests included Mick Jagger, Bertie Hope-Davies, Maurice Craig, Talitha Getty, Marianne Faithfull and Paddy Rossmore.

Desmond at work as Christie's Irish representative at the Birr Castle sale in October 1981.

'Oh, my wife is clever. I'm rather temperamental and she is extremely calm':
Desmond and Olda in the garden at Glin.

Desmond leading his eldest daughter Catherine into the local church for her wedding to actor
Dominic West in June 2010.

Desmond with his first grandchild Dora, daughter of
Catherine FitzGerald and Dominic West.

The Knight of the Women: Desmond in the walled garden at Glin with his wife Olda
and three daughters Catherine, Nesta and Honor.

The library at Glin Castle, still full of objects even after the May 2009 sale.

A passion for the past: Desmond photographed in the entrance hall at Glin before a portrait of his eighteenth-century ancestor John FitzGerald, the 19th Knight.

Jervis' reference to *Irish Furniture* being a 'platform for future studies' is of importance because, as with so much he did, Desmond never saw his work in this field as being the last word on the subject. On the contrary, he wanted to inspire other scholars to undertake further research, to supersede what he had managed to do. 'His real interest,' says Nicholas White, 'was not in personal glory but in the things he was talking and particularly writing about. By handing down information to another generation he was guaranteeing what interested him would continue.'

Irish Furniture's introduction notes pioneering investigation already undertaken in complementary areas by Toby Barnard and Claudia Kinmonth before advising that, within the text, 'We do not discuss in any depth the costs of raw materials and workmanship, and in the virtual absence of bills, we have been unable to work out the individual original worth of the furniture itself. Contemporary attitudes to furniture collecting and its use is an area that still remains to be examined in more detail.' No false claims were being made here; *Irish Furniture* was intended to be a starting point. Other publications would go further.

One of the areas where more work is clearly required concerns the connections between Irish and American furniture. Reviewing the book for the September 2007 issue of *Apollo*, Adam Bowett commented on the problem of national attribution, claiming: 'American scholars have lately seized on details such as the panelled foot as evidence of Irish influence in some parts of North America ... The Philadelphia carver Hercules Courtenay was born in Belfast but trained in London under Thomas Johnson. Does that make his carving Irish? We must distinguish between sound reasoning and wishful thinking.' Desmond would have been delighted if such a distinction could have been decisively established as it had been preoccupying him since he published 'Irish mahogany furniture: A source for American design?' in the April 1971 issue of *Antiques Magazine*. A section of *Irish Furniture* is precisely devoted to inaugurating the disentanglement of Irish from American furniture, a process made all the more difficult by the movement of so much material in the mid twentieth century from one country to the other, and by the absence of documentation in both. Even Bowett allowed that in relation to Irish furniture, shortage of documented pieces was a problem 'and will continue to be so. Without the objective proof of documentation we are left with much that is anecdotal ...'

At least some of that documentation was provided in the book by a directory of all known eighteenth-century Irish furniture makers. This had been compiled by John Rogers who, it will be remembered, almost twenty years earlier had undertaken research into tradesmen of the period based on study of contemporary newspapers. After a decade in the United States, John Rogers had returned to Ireland in 2001 and reconnected with Desmond, who was then getting ready to embark on his book about Irish furniture. Obviously, the material gathered by Rogers was invaluable, especially since he had subsequently tidied it up and put it all on to a computer. 'I went to Glin for two weekends,' he remembers, 'and we went through all my material with a fine-tooth comb. He used some quotes in the main text but then said, "Why don't we use this at the back of the book?"' The resultant directory included many names hitherto unknown to the general public and offered yet more proof of a thriving furniture industry in Ireland during the Georgian period.

Irish Furniture is a major achievement, and a fitting conclusion to Desmond's long-running appraisal of the subject. While it is likely that, as in other fields where he was a trailblazer, fresh research will supplant his own, this should not be regarded as a weakness. Desmond had the tenacity, the verve and the energy to undertake work that had previously attracted little attention, and that mostly of the scornful variety. Thanks to his endeavours, Irish eighteenth-century furniture is now more widely appreciated than has ever been the case since the time of its manufacture. It was this appreciation and understanding that mattered most to him, and that he strove to realize. In their introduction to *Irish Furniture*, Desmond and James Peill wrote:

> We would welcome a major exhibition on Ireland's decorative arts of the eighteenth century, which would include furniture, and would bring together the common threads of the different fields. It would give an overview of the shared patrimony with England and the Continent and show the high level of craftsmanship achieved in Ireland at that time. A show of this stature would waken up the world to a staggering array of art that was manufactured in Ireland during this period.

And so it shall come to pass: in March 2015 a major exhibition devoted to Georgian Ireland's fine and decorative arts is scheduled to open at the Art Institute of Chicago. The show will be dedicated to Desmond's memory and will, without question, result in further reappraisal and research. Just as he wished, the work goes on.

Glin

AT THE END of the introduction to a guidebook about his family home Desmond once wrote, 'It is hoped that Glin Castle, and its collection of family paintings and decorative arts, will be preserved as an example of the social history of an estate in Ireland as seen through the many vicissitudes and changes of fortune of one family over a period of 700 years.'

'The Knight always said Glin was his umbilical chord,' remembers Bob Duff, who came to Glin in 1994. 'He loved Glin with a passion.'

'At the deepest level it was a very emotional attachment,' says Desmond's daughter Catherine. 'Because of the lonely childhood he'd had – he hadn't really had a father – the house, its history and his ancestors, they were real to him. The house was a substitute for family life.'

Love of the family home is scarcely an unusual emotion, especially in Ireland where the passion for land ownership has always been particularly intense. But in our time, few men have done as much not merely to preserve but also to enhance their inheritance as did Desmond. In the February 1990 edition of American *House & Garden*, Olda wrote that after she and Desmond moved to Glin, 'I soon discovered that this house on the banks of the Shannon would always be my greatest rival for my husband's affections.' 'These houses are stern mistresses,' Desmond told Brighid McLaughlin of the *Sunday Independent* in May 1992, 'they own you, take you over, munch you up.'

Yet he submitted willingly to the demands of his exigent mistress. 'His feeling for Glin was enormous,' says Paddy Rossmore. 'Often people feel they're not necessarily cut out for the world into which they're born, but Desmond was absolutely comfortable in his.' Not just comfortable, but determined to make sure that world survived and thrived. Throughout the 1940s and 1950s, the young Desmond had witnessed many similar houses in Limerick and surrounding counties being either abandoned or demolished. Souvenirs from some of those buildings found their way to Glin, chimney pieces in the main rooms and other items elsewhere about the building and grounds. While his own home was the beneficiary of these losses to Ireland's architectural heritage, he was always aware the same fate could yet befall Glin. Following his return to Ireland in 1975, Desmond was witness to, and in his role as Christie's representative a participant in, the breaking up of many house collections, beginning with the Malahide Castle sale of May 1976. He had too often seen the disposal of everything from family portraits to servants' hall china to countenance the idea that such a scenario might be repeated at Glin.

The memory of those lost houses haunted him and more than once he commented that his greatest dread was 'the striped marquee on the lawn' and the scattering of all the house held. This had almost happened in 1803 following the death of the extravagant 23rd Knight, when most of Glin's contents were auctioned. 'Leaving Glin would have been an absolute disaster for him,' says Catherine FitzGerald. 'His identity was so bound up in it, who he was. Glin gave him his whole backbone and raison d'être, his identity was inseparable from it, it all fitted in with his life, his interest in Glin fed into all his other interests.' Indeed, Glin and Desmond were so bound together it was impossible to think of one without the other. He certainly could not do so. Instead, he set out to demonstrate that the survival of an Irish historic house was feasible, to offer owners of other such properties an example of how an apparent anachronism could not simply endure but also thrive in a world quite different from that which had seen its creation. If this meant having to open doors to the public, to rent all or part of the building to a succession of wealthy Americans, to transform the house into a luxury hotel, then

The Knight of Glin, Desmond Fitzgerald with his wife, Lady Olda outside their family seat.

The knight-life of a cultural crusader

IN THE popular imagination, the title Knight conjures up war, armour and medieval fiefdoms, damsels in distress and mailed horses.

However in these parts the title is peculiar to the old fighting Norman aristocracy of Deas Mumhan, South Munster. At any rate it is a title which hardly sits with the genteel pursuits of the arts.

Desmond Fitzgerald however, the 29th Knight of Glin, with a degree in fine art form Harvard has an intense and all consuming interest in the arts. The 29th Knight of Glin is as he readily admits a 'rara avis'. He is also the last of the old English ascendancy world "although we were here a lot longer – since the 13th century to be precise".

The legacy of that old ascendancy world is huge. It is a very visual and visible heritage from famine walls to house styles to castles to municipal and administrative buildings, to parkland and paintings.

in the 17th and 18th centuries and of which his family has many fine examples – painting, furniture, architecture, glass, plate and so on – are raised from neglect.

"At any rate, it is interesting to study things that have been neglected," says Desmond Fitzgerald, who is as keen to show off the restoration of his cobbled courtyard as to talk about things erudite.

Desmond Fitzgerald's 1994 book, The Water Colours of Ireland, which was a survey of three centuries of Irish painting and drawing won a top award for artistic works.

The book was prepared in collaboration with Anne Crookshank.

And now the Knight is working on a book on Irish fine furniture of the 18th and

to put red brick paving in Listowel, which was "quite out of character".

He also keeps a watchful eye on windows in Georgian buildings, keeping a weather-eye open for any unsightly PVC windows.

"They are quite wrong. Wooden sash windows are just as easy to handle and to make."

Right now he is working with Peter Murray of Cork's Crawford Municipal Art Gallery to bring an exhibition of Irish water- colours and drawings from private and municipal collections to America, he lectures to young auctioneers, and he is the representative for Christies, the fine art auction house.

"I deal with material culture, with what is often considered the colonial

try than are leaving it now. I do less and less work for Christies," he says.

He is instead using up his free time working with the University of Limerick on setting up a new degree in fine art and architecture. "The new degree course will be a nice balance to the buzz studies of business and technology at the college.

"Limerick is waking up. It is so nice to see this," he states. The restoration of the Custom House, which will house the Hunt Collection, is something the Knight was very keen to see.

There is no clanking of mail with this knight. Like Chaucer's knight he is indeed a knightly knight – 'a very parfait gentil knight' – courteous and mild mannered with an abiding interest in beauty from his walled garden to his plate, to his heavily polished wooden furniture.

During the summer he is confined to the wing of his castle to make way for paying guests (read rich Americans) to lounge around the

> 'The new course will be a nice balance to the buzz studies of business and technology'

A newspaper article from July 1996 is one of many in which Desmond sought to draw attention to the ongoing threat of dissipation to the national heritage: 'It is important to hang onto all of this.'

so be it: the only alternative hitherto presented had been defeat and departure. Desmond had no intention that this should happen at Glin.

'I think Glin was a great thing for him in getting his bearings,' says Desmond's friend from his time at Harvard, Nelson Aldrich. 'It steadied him, it was his purpose in love to a certain degree. His love of Glin was at the heart of his being.' 'Desmond was absolutely caught up by Glin,' confirms Mark Girouard. 'It was the biggest thing in his life – the idea of keeping it going and learning more about it, too.' Likewise Christopher Gibbs observed Desmond's ardour

> for the white battlemented castle, for the silvery Shannon and the green hills of Clare across it, for the battered castle of his forbears down in the town, for O'Shaugnessy's pub and for the people of Glin, his neighbours and friends, some few of whom were kin, descendants of those sired by his rakehell ancestors, spelling their name with a small g and known as the Knights' makings. Indeed, surveying a crowd of his friends and neighbours he was heard to remark: 'Descended from princes every one of them.'

Desmond always felt himself to be Irish. 'Ireland's immediate impact on me is irresistible,' he declared in the December 1969 issue of *House & Garden*. 'I suppose because from childhood I was brought up here and my blood is still stirred and my imagination bewitched by the tales and folklore of a district where my family has lived continuously for over eight hundred years.' 'He had a tremendous feeling for Ireland,' according to Paddy Rossmore. 'He definitely had an understanding of the country beyond the norm.' In July 1990, Desmond told *Hello!* magazine: 'I do feel extremely Irish. My family all spoke Gaelic until the end of the last century, although I'm afraid I can't speak it myself.' 'I feel totally Irish,' he wrote in the book *Untold Stories: Protestants in the Republic of Ireland 1922–2002*, 'not that I think anything of nationalism – it has caused – is causing – so much grief in the world. Am I accepted here? I feel part of Ireland but I'm not sure Ireland knows what to do with me and my tribe.'

Given the FitzGeralds' long association with this part of the country, Desmond's devotion is understandable. The complicated origins and history of the Knights of Glin have been well documented, not least in an enormous volume on the subject published under the auspices of the Glin Historical Society in 2009. The family can trace its descent from Maurice fitz Gerald, son of Gerald fitz Walter of Windsor and his wife the Welsh Princess Nesta. In 1169, Maurice participated with Richard de Clare, Earl of Pembroke (otherwise known as Strongbow) in the Norman invasion of Ireland and remained in the country. His grandson John fitz Thomas, forebear of the mighty Earls of Desmond, greatly expanded the family territory, especially in the regions of Kerry and West Cork, before being killed with his legitimate son Maurice at the Battle of Callann in 1261. It is now widely accepted that John fitz Thomas had a number of illegitimate offspring, one of whom was John fitz John, founder of the Glin line. His was one of three lines of Knights who appear around this time – the Knights of Glin (or 'Black Knight') and of Kerry (or 'Green Knight'), and 'the White Knight' – the two other titles originating with his siblings or their descendants.

On the other hand, as Christopher Gibbs has remarked:

> None of this story rests on very sound ground, much of it from the chronicle of Nesta's grandson, the historian known as Giraldus Cambrensis who to quote a later historian was the author of absurd eulogiums lauding the Geraldines. Anyway, this extraordinary tribe of ruthless and resourceful warriors produced two main streams, the Kildare FitzGeralds now led by the Duke of Leinster, and the Desmond FitzGeralds represented by the FitzMaurices, Marquesses of Lansdowne, by the Glin FitzGeralds and by the Green Knight or Knight of Kerry.

As for the title Knight of Glin, it has been proposed this was bestowed on John fitz John by his kinsman John fitz Thomas who, in 1316, was ennobled as 1st Earl of Kildare (and was accordingly ancestor of the Dukes of Leinster). Thereafter, the Knighthood of Glin was inherited by prescriptive right. It was not, however, recognized in the British peerage: an attempt in 1814 to have all three Knights' titles officially recognized was unsuccessful. As *Irish Arts Review* editor John Mulcahy noted after Desmond's death, 'There is no mention of the Knights of Glin in *Debrett's*.' (It was, however, always listed in *Burke's Landed Gentry*.)

The greatest achievement of Desmond's ancestors was that they managed to survive, and to retain at least some of their original lands. As a major sub-lineage and vassalage of the Geraldine house of Desmond, successive bellicose Knights of Glin expanded the territory under their control during the fourteenth and fifteenth centuries so that it eventually ran to some 51,000 acres. Successive Knights of Glin were perforce warriors: it was always a struggle to hold on to their lands the extent of which rose and fell as one generation followed another. Granted Shanid in west Limerick in 1197, the family adopted the motto 'Shanid A Boo', meaning 'Shanid for ever', and this was always their war cry. However, owing to the upheavals experienced in Ireland throughout the sixteenth and seventeenth centuries, the Knights lost much of their authority and property. In the 1560s, for example, the 13th Knight's son was accused of treason and executed. His mother, after witnessing her child's hanging, disembowling and decapitation, is said to have seized his head and drank his blood before gathering up the other remains in a linen shroud and taking them for burial to Lislaughtin Friary, west of Glin. In 1600, the old Glin castle was besieged by Sir George Carew. He captured the 14th Knight's six-year-old son and placed him on top of the English forces' defensive position where he would surely have been killed in any attack. Carew then sent word of this to the Knight who responded that he was virile and his wife strong, and they were therefore in a position to produce many more sons. The child was released but the castle lost.

Yet despite a later Knight supporting the hopeless cause of James II, somehow the family managed to recover both their spirits and at least some of their lands. That they retained any property at all must be regarded as extraordinary, especially since his eighteenth-century ancestors were once described by Desmond as 'an improvident, wild and woolly lot who spent a lot of money'. In 1730, the 19th Knight, John FitzGerald, converted from Roman Catholicism to Anglicanism, a move no doubt prompted by the stringencies of the Penal Code. David Fleming has written: 'The eighteenth century FitzGeralds were at best lukewarm Protestants, who seemed to identify both with their Catholic past and traditions as well as the new Protestant establishment. As such they, like many converts, straddled two worlds.' Each generation had its own distinctive character, commemorated by such names as 'the Duelling Knight', 'the Big Knight', 'the Knight of the Women' and, in the middle of the nineteenth century, 'the Cracked Knight', who lived up to his soubriquet by burning all the family papers.

The one thing these earlier FitzGeralds had in common was that they did not much resemble Desmond, displaying few of his aesthetic sensibilities. Once the days of fighting were past, as he wrote in 1996, 'horses, shooting, fishing, sailing and whiskey were their priorities'. On the other hand, one of them, Colonel John

Bateman FitzGerald, 23rd Knight of Glin, was responsible for building the present Glin Castle around the time of his marriage to the English heiress Margaretta Maria Fraunceis Gwyn. At some point in the seventeenth century, the FitzGeralds had moved from their old, much-besieged and battered castle to a thatched residence called Glin Hall. This was burnt in 1740 and replaced by the long, low building that runs to the west of the present main block. The latter when first constructed had none of its present castellation but was a plain, three-storied house with bows on either side of the main entrance facing the Shannon estuary and three-sided bay windows looking out on the gardens behind. Already burdened with debt when he inherited the estate in 1782, Colonel John was improvident and reckless and so his fine new house, on which it was reported he expended 'six thousand pounds and upwards', remained unfinished.

Although the entrance hall and staircase contain splendid Adamesque plasterwork, the top floor stayed bare: when Mark Girouard wrote of Glin Castle in *Country Life* in March 1964, he noted that the rooms on this storey 'remain to this day with bare stone walls, unpainted pine doors, unfinished dadoes and no ceiling'. So bad were his finances that in the immediate aftermath of the colonel's death in 1803 a house-contents auction was held at Glin in which everything except the pictures and silver was offered for sale. The colonel's son John Fraunceis FitzGerald, 24th Knight, who, like Desmond, inherited aged twelve, added battlements to his father's house and thus entitled it to be called a castle although looking more like a toy fort; he also built the battlemented gates and gothic lodges, and as his soubriquet, 'the Knight of the Women', implies, he helped populate the surrounding region. But money remained a problem and by 1837 the estate consisted of 5837 acres (it continued to shrink and eventually Desmond was left with some 400 acres to farm).

Money, or its absence, remained a problem for the 24th Knight's successors up to and including Desmond. When Queen Victoria offered to revive the earldom of Desmond, the 26th Knight felt obliged to decline on the grounds of poverty. As has been discussed, following her husband's death Veronica FitzGerald struggled to hold on to Glin so that it might be passed to her son once he reached his majority. Unable to find a tenant to take the whole place, by 1953 she was advertising for paying guests. While the money this produced was sufficient to cover daily costs, it was certainly not enough for the structural repairs the house began to need. Her marriage to Ray Milner in 1954 resolved this difficulty, since he provided funds in the region of £60,000 for a restoration programme, beginning with the roof where the old slates were replaced with Canadian shingles. Desmond was always lavish in praise of and appreciation for his stepfather, describing him as 'an extraordinarily sympathetic and benevolent influence on my life'. 'Ray took a vital interest in Glin,' he wrote in 2009, 'and like my mother had fallen in love with the house and was determined to restore it, as by now water was streaming down the walls underneath the battlements as the weight of the old slates was pushing out the walls. All the battlements had to be taken down and rebuilt in order to put it in a string course.'

It was Paddy Healy, estate carpenter and long-time mentor of Desmond, who oversaw this work on the house. He had a long association with Glin, just like Desmond who in the winter 2009 edition of the *Irish Arts Review* wrote:

> Paddy's grandfather, another Paddy, was a master carpenter and was active in the 1880s and also worked at the castle … Paddy told me that his great-grandfather, Thomas Healy, was a turner who with his foot pedal lathe crafted the banisters of Glin's delicate flying stair-case in the 1790s – quite a record of continued tradition in one place. Paddy was proud of this long connection with the castle where he worked so faithfully from a boy of eight with his father, and continued after his father's death as the house carpenter almost until his own death in 1987 – all of 72 years. He remembered clearing up the wood shavings for his father in the immaculate castle workshop and repairing some of the many windows of the castle when starlings had flown into and broken the delicate crown glass.

Had Ray Milner not provided help when he did, the likelihood is that Glin Castle would not be standing today. 'He used to talk about the house,' remembers Nelson Aldrich, 'and he also talked often and with great gratitude and affection about his stepfather. Desmond probably wouldn't have been who he was without his stepfather's support.' Ray Milner not only took care of structural repairs at Glin but also paid for many of the items of furniture and decorative art bought for the house during these years: photographs of the interior from the middle of the last century show how empty were the rooms, never properly filled again after the sale of 1803.

By 1960, however, Ray Milner understandably decided enough of his money had been spent on Glin. Alternative sources of income had to be found to sustain the estate since farming the last few hundred acres did not generate sufficient funds. Once more the decision was taken to let Glin Castle. Now at Harvard, Desmond assumed responsibility for finding a tenant, preferably American, who would be prepared to take Glin for a few years. In February 1961 he wrote to his mother and stepfather: 'I put an advertisement into the *New Yorker* and shall also do so in *Town & Country*. I am going to deal with the situation myself which will save an American agent … The farm really seems still a hideous problem. God I hope we may be able to let the house. You both have been so wonderful about it all.'

Desmond's advertisements caused quite a stir and led to him being widely interviewed; never reluctant to step forward, this may be the origin of his love of the press. 'I can't afford to keep the castle up,' he frankly confessed to the editor of *The Standard-Times*. Not, he hastily added, that the running costs of Glin would be terribly high for any tenant, 'it's just that a graduate student studying for his PhD in fine arts at Harvard University isn't exactly in a position to keep up a castle too.' To a reporter from *The Boston Globe* he advised that Glin was unusual in Ireland because it had six bathrooms and central heating, and said that he had received expressions of interest from throughout the United States and even from a Hollywood film company. In the event, within a few months he had let the castle to a Wall Street financier, Duncan Spencer, for an annual rent of £800, with the proviso that Desmond could reside in the wing for short periods when visiting on agricultural business. This arrangement proved ideal while he was in the United States but less so after Desmond returned to Ireland in May 1963. Before the year ended, the tenants had left and he was once more able to use Glin Castle for himself, and for his many friends.

Desmond loved to entertain and Glin allowed him the opportunity to do so on a larger scale than could most of his contemporaries. Unlike many Irish houses of the period and thanks to Ray Milner's help the building had decent facilities, not least the ample provision of bathrooms. And while it was nowhere near as wonderfully furnished as would later become the case, thanks to the efforts of both Veronica and Desmond Glin's interior decoration was considerably better than it had been even a couple of decades earlier. Since the early 1960s, Desmond frequently filled the house with guests, often more than there were beds. Christopher Gibbs remembers:

Perhaps it was during the Loulou years that Desmond gave a great party at Glin. It was my first glimpse of Ireland and a fine initiation. A London group arrived at Shannon and Garech Browne, Mariga Guinness and Milo Talbot de Malahide led us to Glin, but slowly, because we had to look at Bunratty, where Lord Gort's grand medieval collection was being installed by John and Putzel Hunt, and we had to try and get a glimpse of Mount Ievers, and we had to see whether Dromore had fallen down, and there were all these charming places to have a soothing drink along the way, so it was near six when we showed up at Glin. The Knight was anxious, as these rowdies tumbled into the hall. 'Please don't be rude to my mother,' he begged. 'I've been perfectly civil to the old bugger all my life, why should I start now!' quoth one of our number. At which point the handsome Knight-mère, as we called her, came through the door with an icy welcome. It was the merriest of parties, and many of us men slept in sleeping bags, after a long night of revelry. In the morning we were told to leave after breakfast, and Mariga ferried us back to Leixlip …

According to David Mlinaric, another regular guest from the early 1960s, 'The hospitality at Glin was fantastic. But it was a place of scholarship *and* hospitality, and that was what made it unique.'

Desmond's photograph albums chronicle the extraordinary range of people who came to stay at Glin during this period. A page picked at random from a house party in spring 1970 shows that among the guests were Mick Jagger, Marianne Faithfull, Maurice Craig, Bertie Hope-Davies, Christopher Gibbs, Talitha Getty, Robert Fraser and Paddy Rossmore. The visitors' book at Glin provides further evidence of all those who enjoyed Desmond's hospitality over many decades, some leaving behind more than just their names and dates of visit. Here, for example, are the opening lines of a poem written by one visitor in the early 1960s:

> The marble halls stood silent
> At the bonny Castle Glin
> 'The master's gone to Cambridge town
> Will he n'ae come back agin?'
> Then came young Desmond riding
> With a cry of 'Hang the Debt!'

Back to the wine-dark Shannon
In a constellation jet.

He called for meat and foaming mead
And other, stronger liquor
He called for a minstrel of renown
Whose name was Chubby Checker.

Something about Glin moved many visitors to verse, of varying merits. The
following lines were written by American guests in May 1982:

There's nothing like it, at home or abroad
For to be here and sample their room and board
Is heaven by the Shannon with FitzGerald grace
Surrounded by weather which oft changes face.
So here's to the castle – it's bliss with a view
Hail to FitzGeralds – Shanid Abu!
We lift our glass to that talented two
To Desmond and Olda our best toast to you.

And finally, a piece of self-confessed doggerel from May 2009 by Peter Murray,
director of Cork's Crawford Gallery. The author imagines Glin as a model of Soviet
collectivization and includes the following lines about Desmond:

Citizen Desmond is in charge of the libraries
Biographies, histories, epistles and diaries
Recording for posterity the follies and excesses
Of once all-powerful dukes and duchesses
He catalogues their seats, and also their chairs
Describing their terraces, parks and squares
His interest, of course, not in toffs and nobs
But in the hard-won victories of revolutionary mobs.

Although employed by Christie's soon after he returned to live in Ireland with
his family in the mid 1970s, Desmond still had to generate additional income in

order to maintain Glin. Already in spring 1969 he had converted the main gate lodge into a shop selling Irish goods including clothing made nearby by Hollypark Knitwear, a business in which he was an investor. 'I shall also be serving brown bread, sandwiches, soup of the day and salad,' Desmond told a reporter from the *Daily Express* in May, although he never actually worked in the shop, which was run by the energetic Joan Stack. At the beginning he was optimistic this new venture would make money, despite reservations on the part of his mother and stepfather. 'I still think we were wise to do the shop as it will pick up gradually,' he wrote to them in July, the following month reporting that sometimes up to £100-worth of business was generated in a day, 'but on average the sum is about £40. I have been getting some more publicity done and I really think that once it has been established for a year or so it will go from strength to strength.' Unfortunately, the main road leading from Limerick to County Kerry, which formerly went through Glin and thus brought many tourists to the village, was moved inland in the 1970s. As a consequence the shop ceased to attract sufficient custom and eventually closed.

Meanwhile, the castle was once more offered for rent. When Desmond's mother had tried to find tenants in the early 1950s there had been no takers. Now the market was better and every summer Glin was taken, usually by various American visitors who would occupy the entire main block. 'Of course, all Desmond's American connections were good,' says Olda. 'He understood what they wanted and how it worked.' Guests were looked after by Nancy Ellis and Una Bourke, both of whom had worked in Glin since Desmond was a small child, the latter beginning as his nursemaid. Their long-standing association with and devotion to the house delighted visitors: in November 1987, Australian *Vogue*'s Marion von Adlerstein took more notice of the two women than she did of Desmond and Olda:

> As Nancy showed us into the smoking room after dinner at Glin Castle, she told us fondly about a woman from Texas who rents the castle for a few weeks every summer. She is adored by the staff because she sends the rest of her party away on day trips – riding, fishing, shopping, sightseeing – but never moves from the castle. She savours every moment.

'One has to look for new perspectives on how to keep things going,' Desmond commented to *Hello!* in July 1990, 'and after all this house was built for entertaining, so to me it's a very great pleasure to see it full of people.' During these periods he and Olda, along with their children, moved into a section of the old wing, sharing just a handful of rooms. This was the norm for more than twenty years and one accepted by all the family. Not everyone would wish to hand over their house to strangers, even if only temporarily, but Desmond and his wife and children all understood they had to do so if Glin was to be retained. Their mutual love for Glin was always tempered by a streak of pragmatism. 'It was quite normal, really,' Catherine FitzGerald remembers. 'In the summer there were guests, and we lived in the wing. He loved going up and telling them stories and showing them the house. He absolutely loved talking to people.'

In addition, there would be groups of people coming to visit the house, perhaps just for a tour, perhaps for lunch or dinner. If he were on the premises, invariably they could expect to be entertained by Desmond whose pleasure in speaking of his family history, its association with the region, and the house occupied by genera-tions of ancestors never waned. 'He delights in the tourists' delight,' reported Tim Willis in *The Times* in September 1990,

> as he explains the significance of the ornate plasterwork, with its cornu-copiae and constellations, harp and horns. No matter how many times, he still enjoys telling how the hall chairs were carved to form an impromptu cockfighting ring; how this is the very sword with which 'The Duellist' – the 21st Knight – stuck a dastardly Spaniard in the neck.

Determined to make sure the charms of Glin were as widely known as possible, Desmond became adept at finding fresh ways to generate publicity for the house. Journalists were encouraged to stay and to savour the history of Glin and its contents, preferably under Desmond's tutelage. 'It takes some time to familia-rise ourselves with the castle hall,' rhapsodized the *Sunday Times*' Cal McCrystal in May 1988, 'the Irish oak and walnut furniture, the flying staircase, the secret library doors and a houseful of treasures and lore – about "the Cracked Knight" who damaged his brain falling off a horse, "the Knight of the Women" fluent in Gaelic and sex, "the Big Knight" fond of the bottle. The present knight is often one's personal guide.'

And so he continued to be for those fortunate enough to be invited to stay at Glin where, as Christopher Gibbs wrote in the January 1995 issue of *House & Garden*, at the close of each rental season

> friends from London days, local gentry and well known architects feast on rural plenty, washed down with knightly claret. Local wonders are explored in brilliantly orchestrated picnics: the party may chug out to Cannon Island, or gather the sacred mushrooms of holy Scattery in the mouth of the Shannon. We are shown Godwin's gaunt ruin at Dromore; we hunt the banshee at Lough Gur; we plunge into seaweed baths at Ballybunion. Pop stars and politicians, diplomats, decorators, scholars and merchants, poets, botanists and grandees, all whirl in the Glin fandango …

Any surplus money made from letting the house was put back into the building and improving its appearance. 'It was all fairly dingy,' he told me in May 2007 when speaking about the Glin of his youth. 'Most of the original contents had been sold a long time ago. There was a mahogany sideboard in the hall – it's still there – and, in the back hall, a Regency sideboard probably made for the house in Cork around 1820.' Desmond could not consider leaving the place in that condition and so over half a century he, first alone and then with Olda's help, devoted enormous quantities of time to beautifying the house he had inherited.

Olda's particular focus was the gardens, which, by the time she arrived, were suffering from long neglect. The 2.5-acre early-nineteenth-century walled garden, for example, had become overgrown and no longer used as a source for fresh fruit and vegetables. Walls here were repaired, walkways recreated, arched openings refurbished and the walled garden made once more into a model of its kind. As Patrick Bowe wrote in *Country Life* in January 1997, a historic walled garden can be one of an historic property's most substantial efforts. 'Now that this inestimable value has been realised at Glin Castle, the kitchen garden could be on its way to regaining its popularity as a working feature of the country estate.' Elsewhere in the pleasure grounds, old features were rediscovered and restored, just as new ones were created, while an abundance of planting was undertaken. Improvement at Glin took place as much outdoors as in, and once more offered other Irish estate owners an example of what could be achieved with sufficient determination and flair.

Stasis was never an option. *The Times'* Tim Willis reported in September 1990 that Desmond constantly improved and changed and added to Glin, each year setting himself a task, the next being the replacement of the carpet on the main staircase, 'even though my daughter says it will make the place look like an hotel'. In September 1996 he told an American journalist: 'We had the windows repainted last year. It cost twelve thousand pounds just to paint the windows.' At the same time, Desmond the incorrigible collector was forever acquiring additional items of Irish interest: furniture, pictures, ceramics; the greater part of which were placed about the castle. Many of these items have been discussed in an earlier chapter. They were so cleverly arranged by Desmond and Olda that visitors unfamiliar with the house invariably gained the impression that this showcase of Irish craftsmanship had been in place for hundreds of years. Glin, declared John Cornforth in *Country Life* in June 1998, 'is an unusual collector's house because it does not feel like one: everything looks as though it has always been there, and recent arrivals are completely at ease with the ancestors. So, without the Knight as guide, no one could guess how everything has come together.'

Yet, as Olda wrote in the February 1990 issue of American *House & Garden*,

> Glin is not a decorator's dream. Never completely done over, it is instead
> a house that has gradually grown together, room by room, to become a
> living page out of the history of Irish artists and craftsmen ... Every wall
> is plastered with paintings of Irish subjects by Irish painters like a foreign
> envelope with stamps: some of these we have brought from places as far
> away as New South Wales and Vancouver Island.

In this respect, Desmond and Olda were highly unusual; the customary trend for owners of country houses is to dispose of contents, gradually divesting the interiors of the works of art accumulated by previous generations. At Glin the opposite was the case: not a year went by without some part of the building gaining further items. The result, as Desmond often commented, was that Glin became a repository of Irish painting and the decorative arts, a rare opportunity to see how such houses would have looked hundreds of years ago and what one commentator called 'a unique teaching tool'. 'No Irish museum or country house presents such an integrated view of the 18th and early 19th centuries as the Knight has developed at Glin,' observed John Cornforth in the same *Country Life* article. 'It has been – and continues to be – a voyage of discovery for him but one he has always shared … He has helped to create the enthusiasm for things Irish which is one of the great changes of the past 40 years. This has grown out of Glin, a place that never lets the Knight or his wife rest.'

The improvement of his inheritance was a lifetime's project, a never-ending work in progress and an act of cultural bravado. As the number of Irish historic houses still owned by their original families continued to dwindle, Desmond defied the trend and made Glin lovelier than it had ever been in the past. Ultimately, this led him to do something none of his forebears, despite their greater disposable incomes, had managed to achieve: the completion of Glin Castle's top floor.

At the time of the 23rd Knight's death in 1803, only the ground and first floor of his newly built house had been finished. There followed the catastrophic sale and the second storey was not fitted out. This remained the case for almost two centuries. In the spring of 1980, Olda offered an eloquent description of the castle's top floor as it still was:

> Room after room was never finished. The bare brick walls are laced at intervals with strange shapes. What looks like an oeuil de boeuf window. An arch here, a fireplace there: all bricked in. Architectural historians get out their measuring tapes and scratch their pates. A wonderful long room the width of the house has floorboards with gaping holes, with the bare bones of the roof rising above it. The windows have their original green bubbly glass. Strange collections of objects have been left behind or stored against the future in curious-looking lumpy groups. There is a graveyard of old hoovers; a selection of dusty, incredibly slim hunting boots. Every sort and shape of basket. Tin trunks, old wash stands and jugs.

Sixteen years later in *The World of Hibernia* Desmond wrote of the same space as it was about to disappear: 'pine doors unpainted, walls only partially plastered, and an absence of ceilings, which left exposed the oak beams and rafters. Cornices were only partially in place and a marble mantelpiece was set up in an otherwise totally unfinished room.'

The decision to finish the house's top floor was taken after New Zealander Bob Duff came to work in the house in October 1994, initially as a cook for periods when the whole premises was being rented. 'Una and Nancy really had to retire,' Olda explains, 'and Sally Phipps said Bob might be looking for a job.' He remembers the following summer being not only incredibly hot but also exceptionally good in terms of finding tenants: 'Don Keough, who had been president of Coca-Cola, rented Glin for the whole of August.' Desmond and Olda felt more could be done with the house, but they were unsure what. 'We used to let the house every summer,' she says, 'but lets weren't cutting the mustard, they just weren't generating enough money.' Darina Allen of Ballymaloe House, County Cork, was an old friend and she suggested Desmond and Olda consult Geraldine Fitzgerald and Bert Allen of the Bewley's Hotel Group who, Bob Duff recalls, 'came and said we could make a bit of a go of the place as a hotel'.

It was not the first time such an idea had been mooted. In April 1809 when the 25th Knight was still a minor, Glin was offered for rent, a notice in the *Limerick Chronicle* advising prospective tenants that 'a proper person that would open a hotel there for the Summer Season will meet with every encouragement'. Almost 190 years later this notion came to pass. In 1997–8, Glin's hitherto neglected top floor was transformed into five bedroom suites, while on the first floor another bedroom was created, meaning there were now twelve in the main house, plus a further three in the nearest part of the wing. Enormous amounts of other work on the building were carried out during the late 1990s, much of it done by the next generation of the same Healy family that had been associated with the estate for generations and maintained the necessary craftsmanship.

'We didn't just do up the top floor,' says Bob Duff.

> There was a new roof, and a new Venetian window inserted above the plaster ceiling of the staircase. A proper commercial kitchen was installed; a whole laundry. The whole house was rewired and replumbed, and a new boiler installed: the old one had been put in in the late 1920s and gave enough hot water for about two baths. The winter of 1998 was terrible, we were five days without power and lost everything in the freezer, so put in our own generator. A well was drilled and a filtration system installed. The most tremendous amount of work was done on the place.

All the bedrooms were beautifully furnished with antiques, the walls covered in hand-blocked paper from Irish specialist David Skinner, the curtains and bed hangings often made from old fabrics. As elsewhere in the house, it was impossible to tell what had been there for centuries and what newly acquired; all blended into an harmonious whole. Outdoors, Olda and her eldest daughter Catherine worked on further transforming the gardens to make them every bit as splendid as the house. 'It was his dream,' says Olda. 'To show how a country house would have been furnished in the eighteenth century with Irish furniture and paintings and all of that.' Desmond now realized the dream and at the same time gave new life to his family home, filling it with guests albeit some of them paying. 'He sort of curated the main house and kept it almost like a museum,' says Catherine. 'He wanted to show it to people and explain to them that was how he saw the Irish house.' Although it operated as a hotel, Glin continued to give the impression of being a private house. 'The funny thing is we never lost anything,' Olda remarks. 'Bob was a marvellous manager.'

'We opened by St Patrick's Day,' Bob Duff explains, 'and closed around mid-November. Every penny made was ploughed back into Glin. Other hotels had spas and swimming pools and golf; we just had Glin and its contents, so we had to make it work on the basis of the house and the quality of service.' Desmond and Olda were completely committed to making sure the enterprise was a success. 'He just loved having the house full of people,' Bob Duff comments. 'When Desmond was there he would go up every night before dinner and meet the guests.'

With the main house set up as an hotel, Desmond and the rest of the family now made the wing into their permanent residence, completely refurbishing it to create more comfortable quarters for themselves, including a large first-floor sitting room with walls covered in densely packed bookshelves. When the season ended, they would invite friends to visit Glin just as had always been the case. Desmond and Olda's hospitality was justifiably renowned, as countless letters of thanks testify. As far back as May 1975 – when they had only just returned to Ireland and Desmond was still recovering from his breakdown – author Robert Graves could write, 'You gave us a wonderful time at Glin ... We were so gratefully impressed by all the work you did in your splendid ancient castle, you treated us with the most enchanted and modern nobility.'

Ten years later, Molly Keane's daughter Sally Phipps wrote to Olda after a stay at Glin: 'You and Desmond are wonderful, imaginative hosts and it is something

I really admire you both for. You never stop looking after people, which requires constant feats of energy and yet you never show tiredness and always have time for conversation and jokes.' Another decade on, and Susan Kellett of Enniscoe, County Mayo, exclaimed:

> I can't thank you enough for such a delightful visit. Wonderful to see Glin and all its treasures, great comfort and delicious food, and the many entertaining people of such variety and diversity of interests. My head was still in a whirl after I arrived back at Enniscoe. You are both marvellous to keep it all going, not just going but developing all the time.

'You have just given Val and me the most wonderful, *wonderful* treat,' enthused garden designer Helen Dillon in November 1997. 'There couldn't be anywhere nicer in the world to stay than at Glin. Unbelievably comfortable rooms, all so prettily done up ... I know you know it, but the house has incredible charm, down to the tiniest detail.'

'Glin was wonderful,' wrote Mark Girouard in November 1999, almost forty years after he had first come to stay in the house, 'such luxury – such succulence – such service – such company!' 'Where to begin?' wondered writer and broadcaster Polly Devlin after staying with Desmond and Olda in November 2004.

> At the beginning, into the house glimmering with light and colour, blazing fires & drinking the best champagne. And it went on from there – sensational in every sense. I cannot think when I enjoyed anything more. And there was *so* much to enjoy. New people who were wonderful; what has happened at Glin: those walks, the new vistas, the plantings, the comfort of the house, the deliciousness of the food.

One could quote similar exclamations of pleasure and gratitude from countless letters sent to Glin by anyone fortunate to have stayed there during this period. The house looked lovelier than ever, was better run and more meticulously maintained, and filled with people who delighted in all that Desmond and Olda had achieved and felt privileged to share it, if only temporarily.

'Really the years from 1998 to 2008 were fantastic,' Bob Duff remembers. 'And then it all changed.' The global economic downturn affected Glin's business with extraordinary rapidity. '2006 was our best year ever,' remembers Olda. 'The volume of people started to dry up in 2007 and then just stopped in 2008. We only had fifteen bedrooms, it wasn't very big and if not filled regularly then it just wasn't feasible.' Bob Duff used to travel to the United States, from whence came the majority of the house's paying guests. When he made one of these trips in December 2008, the impact of economic recession was instantly and widely apparent: 'I went to this really expensive shopping mall in Denver and there was nobody in it. Our market just vanished. I came back to Glin and said to Desmond, "Close".' 'Because people were booking later,' Desmond afterwards remembered, 'we kept hoping they'd come, but they never did. We just had to grapple the bull by the horns.'

After expending so much time, effort and money on refurbishing and estab-lishing Glin as a small luxury hotel, the decision to close was not taken lightly. Perversely, as Bob Duff notes, the building had never been in as good condition as when it shut for business. 'It's all done up,' Desmond commented to me at the time. 'Anyone could just walk in, turn on the cooker and away they'd go.' On the other hand, remaining open was not an option. The staff had to be made redun-dant (thankfully, Bob Duff worked hard to make sure most of them found jobs elsewhere) and the greater part of the main house mothballed. Although this was obviously a blow, Desmond and Olda remained resolutely pragmatic. 'The hotel had stopped working,' she says. 'Visitors stopped coming and we needed something else to bring in an income: the care and maintenance of the house demanded that.' 'You have to take steps,' Desmond said when we spoke of the matter around this time. 'You can't just lock up the house, it's like having a difficult and demanding child on your hands.'

The 'something else' on which Desmond and Olda settled was a sale of many items of furniture and fine art that he had collected over the previous forty-plus years. 'When we came to that stage,' says Bob Duff, who was still working at Glin in a part-time capacity, 'the stage of wondering what would keep the place going, Desmond was very sanguine. I was expecting fireworks but he took it all extremely well.' Once he had resolved that the best way to ensure the house's future was to dispose of some of its contents, Desmond moved with speed. Held in Christie's King Street rooms in London on 7 May 2009, 'Glin Castle: A Knight in Ireland' featured 200 lots of furniture, pictures, porcelain and silver. As with any other auction with which he had been involved, Desmond was determined this one would be a success.

Instead of allowing himself grow despondent at the thought of a lifetime's treasures being dispersed, he focused on ensuring the sale received ample publicity. 'One of the points my father always made about Desmond,' says Ted Clive of Christie's, 'was that he was tremendously honest about the struggle to keep up Glin. So when it came to the sale, he was intensely practical about everything.' 'It's very sad and a big shock,' he told me not long before the auction. 'It means selling my collection which I've enjoyed and written about, but it hasn't upset me too much.' As has already been remarked, Desmond bought and sold almost from childhood, regularly seeking opportunities to dispose of one item even while acquiring another. The Christie's auction could therefore be seen as simply another moment in a lifetime's trading. 'Country-house sales were very much his thing,' comments Nicholas White of Christie's. 'And he was always a bit of a trader. When it came to the Glin sale, he almost curated it; his timing was brilliant.'

Although the majority of lots were pieces that Desmond had bought over the previous few decades, the sale also included a certain amount of family silver that had rarely been used, and a couple of items of furniture. But the greater part of it represented Desmond's own collecting habits. 'The sale was a celebration of his taste and his brilliant choice,' observes Olda. 'He'd always been very cool about objects and things: he knew with a sixth sense when was the right time to sell something.' Catherine likewise comments that her father was 'so matter of fact' about the sale, accepting its necessity, refusing to become despondent. What mattered was that each lot carried the correct attribution and as much information about provenance as possible. In a way, the sale catalogue, with an eloquent introduction by William Laffan celebrating Desmond's perspicacity and erudition, became another of his books. Like them it promoted the merits of Irish craftsmanship and encouraged greater interest in the country's fine and decorative arts.

'He adored the sale,' Olda remembers. 'Christie's gave us this huge lunch party, and he and Miss Crookshank gave a talk.' There was terrific interest and as a result prices often exceeded pre-auction estimates. The occasion was a validation of Desmond's discernment, which explains why he adopted such a positive approach to the scattering of his treasures. Meanwhile back at Glin, assisted by Ted Clive and

Orlando Rock, head of private collections at Christie's, Desmond rearranged the main rooms so that anyone not intimately familiar with the house would never have known a single item had been removed. 'It's rather nice meeting pieces of one's furniture in other people's houses,' Olda now says. 'It makes one realize one can't own things because their life goes on when one's own comes to an end.' It is also worth noting that in the handful of years since, whenever any lot from the Glin auction has come on the market this provenance has served as a mark of distinction, enhancing the value of the item in question. And while it was tough parting with so many carefully collected objects, their sale did mean the house itself was not in jeopardy.

Hardly was the auction over than Desmond had moved on to his next project: the publication of a substantial monograph on the history of the FitzGeralds of Glin. Many other, more prominent Irish families must envy the amount of attention Desmond's forbears have received. He had always been passionately interested in his ancestors, yet their study suffered from two drawbacks: from the late seventeenth century on, none of them had been especially notable in public life; and the greater part of the family archive was lost, believed to have been burnt by the 25th or 'Cracked Knight' in the 1860s. 'As a small boy,' Desmond wrote, 'I was always trying to discover any stories about the place and put some flesh on the meagre Glin FitzGerald family tree. Considering the antiquity of the family there was at this time comparatively little known about what they did and what they were like.' When Desmond embarked in adulthood on serious exploration of the family into which he had been born, there was little material available to him other than occasional references to earlier Knights in the files of the *Limerick Chronicle*, first published in 1768.

Fortunately, the Knights of Glin had fascinated several enthusiastic historians, particularly those from the immediate locality. One of them, Thomas F. Culhane who had emigrated to Melbourne in 1927, collected a great deal of folklore and factual information about the FitzGeralds even though living on the other side of the planet. This he willingly shared with Desmond in the late 1950s. In 1978, the Listowel-born priest and author Fr J. Anthony Gaughan was able to draw on Culhane's research when he published his own history, *The Knights of Glin*, which also included an examination of the family's genealogy, a study of the names of townlands in Glin, a list of poems in Irish associated with the Knights and a discussion of Glin Castle and its contents by Desmond.

Nevertheless, the opportunity remained for a more detailed investigation and in autumn 2009 *The Knights of Glin: Seven Centuries of Change* appeared. A large handsome illustrated volume running to more than 460 pages, it was published under the auspices of the Glin Historical Society with erudite contributions by many of that body's members as well as by academic scholars. There were also sections written by Desmond on his family, and by Olda on the gardens at Glin. As Patrick Skene Catling remarked in a *Spectator* review in January 2010, 'In this splendid, monumental slab of a book, Desmond FitzGerald, 29th Knight of Glin, has made the chronicle of his family epitomize the whole turbulent history of Ireland since the arrival of the Normans.' This was perhaps the greatest triumph of the book: it integrated the tale of Desmond's family with that of the country, making the two indistinguishable. And it served as a fitting culmination to Desmond's decades-long investigation into FitzGerald lore: almost everything that could be learnt about his predecessors was now gathered within the same covers. Just as he had made Glin Castle into a treasury of Irish taste in the Georgian period, so he made the history of the FitzGeralds embody that of an entire class. Yet again Desmond was a trailblazer, showing what could be achieved with modest resources provided sufficient determination and persistence were brought to the undertaking.

The Knights of Glin: Seven Centuries of Change rightly received enthusiastic reviews, many of which declared it a model of local studies that could and should be emulated elsewhere and by other families. Perhaps the most eloquent tribute paid to the book came from Nobel Laureate Seamus Heaney, who in March 2010 wrote to Desmond:

> The book is a beautiful act of pietà and a mighty act of scholarship, and in your own contributions the combination of love (of people, of place) and learning (historical, art-historical, general) make for a volume that is more than a compendium … It is a work to be extolled and a gift we shall cherish – and I'm proud to be cited at the end of your fond and richly informative chapter on that 'volatile existence' of the castle, owner and contents. The physical volume is magnificent – heartbreakingly attractive with all those photos and pictures and maps and landscapes – worthy to be raised like a missal on an altar and held above the brow of some kneeling acolyte for the Knight to gaze upon and contemplate – as WBY might put it – 'in excited reverie!'

Desmond was rightly proud of this accolade. Harry Mount declared in *Country Life* that *The Knights of Glin* 'is a jolly *festschrift* to the 29 Knights' and to Desmond in particular. Patrick Bowe wrote in *The Irish Times* that 'if Ireland were Japan, the present and 29th Knight of Glin might be classified as "a living national monument"'. There was a sense the book marked the conclusion of a lifetime's work, and indeed this proved to be the case: by the time *The Knights of Glin* came out, Desmond was already suffering from the cancer that led to his death two years later.

It is a paradox that Desmond gave little consideration to two interrelated matters, which, with his passionate interest in family history and in Glin Castle, one might have thought would be of paramount concern: the absence of a male heir, and the future of the house he had done so much to preserve and beautify. Interviewed by *Irish Arts Review* editor John Mulcahy for the magazine's winter 2003 issue, Desmond was quizzed about the fact that he had no son. 'The title has always gone down in the male line,' he coolly responded, 'as indeed have all the successions among Irish chiefs.' The male line concluded with Desmond but he was unperturbed. 'I cannot really feel too sad about that,' he remarked to *Hello!* magazine in July 1990. 'A male heir would have inherited an impossible burden, and I could not see it surviving in its present form for another generation.' This wasn't affectation or bravado: Desmond truly spoke as he felt.

The subject of succession to his ancient title, or rather the lack thereof, seems to have troubled observers more than it did him. Writing in the *Sunday Independent* in May 1992, Brighid McLaughlin commented: 'The sense of mortality must be all-engulfing. I watched him carefully to see if he was feigning indifference but he genuinely seemed not to mind. This is hard to believe and does not fit in with his historic and humanistic perceptions. He repeats that it does not worry him in the least.' Ten years later when asked by Victoria Mary Clarke in the same newspaper if he felt sad to be the last Knight of Glin, he unhesitatingly answered: 'No, because it's time there was an end to it. It's just a romantic charade.' And again in the *Sunday Independent*, a publication strangely preoccupied with the issue, Desmond declared that 'The Knight of Glin is a romantic title. It's not much use except for the romance of the story.'

Of course, since the Knighthood of Glin is not governed by the same rules as a title awarded by the British crown, it could be continued, perhaps by skipping a generation. 'It always seemed to me quite unnecessary that he should be the last Knight,' says Mark Girouard. 'It's a title of no rules, so why shouldn't his grandson be the next Knight of Glin?' In general, Desmond's friends preferred not to discuss the absence of a future 30th Knight with the last holder. 'I never did,' says Eddie McParland who believes that 'one of the reasons he didn't feel sorry was because that would have involved him saying he was sorry his daughters weren't boys'. This was far from being the case. In the early nineteenth century, the amatory 24th Knight had been known as 'the Knight of the Women'. The same title might have been applied to Desmond since he contentedly lived in the company of his wife and three daughters.

'Luckily I like women very much,' he wrote in 2004, 'and have always been extremely fond of them.' According to Catherine, 'He'd say, "Oh, I think a son would have been a disaster and I much prefer girls." There was no pain in the soul: once it hadn't happened, he just got on with it. He seemed perfectly happy being the 29th and last Knight.'

In the winter 2003 edition of the *Irish Arts Review*, John Mulcahy suggested Desmond take cognisance of the Irish Republic's equal-rights legislation, to which he received the diplomatic reply: 'There are many stimulating changes in the world today and your suggestion certainly has merit.' Yet Desmond never took action to ensure there would be a 30th Knight; other concerns took precedence. 'I was upset,' comments Olda, 'because people were always saying, "Oh, no Knights of Glin in the future." But he didn't mind, I think he loved being the Knight of Glin. "Where is Plantagenet now?" he would ask, pointing out lots of other families hadn't had sons.'

In July 1990, Desmond told *Hello!* magazine: 'My main concern is to ensure the preservation of Glin Castle. When I was a curator at the V & A, I had the opportunity of acquiring a lot of Irish artefacts and bringing them here to turn the house into a living museum. I want it to survive.' And yet as has been shown, finding a means to guarantee Glin's survival was a challenge throughout his entire life. 'It was built as a show-off house and has been difficult for everyone ever since,' Catherine points out. 'To make the house sustainable has always been a problem.' Desmond hoped that either Glin would be commercially viable or that some institution would take over responsibility for its maintenance and wellbeing. 'Of course, I would wish to continue the family's close involvement with this ancient patrimony,' he told

Hello! in the same interview, 'even if the house is turned over to other, perhaps educational uses. Glin Castle will withstand, even without a Knight.'

In the years immediately following, the solution appeared to be: run Glin as a small luxury hotel. After that venture closed in 2008, it seems that Desmond entertained hopes the newly established Irish Heritage Trust might take on the house. This aspiration perforce disappeared when the government announced in December 2008 that it would not be providing the IHT with financial support, which had earlier been promised. News of the state's change of heart came six months before items from Glin were sold by Christie's and was most likely partly responsible for that event. Speaking of the withdrawal of promised financial support to the IHT, Desmond told me 'that was the knell, really. Now I just hope we can weather the storm and stay at Glin; we're looking into various hopeful possibilities.' While Desmond was saddened an organization he had helped bring into being and for which he entertained high hopes was rendered considerably less effective than intended, 'He never talked about his disappointment,' says Catherine. 'He never got embittered, after so much campaigning.'

'Glin has been the ancestral property of my family for over 700 years,' Desmond commented at the time of the Christie's sale. 'It is my greatest hope that it will continue to remain in the family and be enjoyed and cherished long into the future.' Yet in the end one has a sense that, like the sale, like the lack of a male heir, he became sanguine about Glin's future and grew to accept that what would be would be. He had fought a good and long fight, and nobody could accuse him of not trying his best. Now there was nothing more he could do, especially as he was battling ill health.

'The awful thing was that he didn't really believe in death,' says Olda. Nor, it seems, in religion. 'No, I don't believe in religion,' he told the *Sunday Independent*'s Victoria Mary Clarke in November 2002. 'When I die I'll be content with having achieved something in this life. I don't need to make plans for another one.' Anyone who saw Desmond during his last two years will remember how disease physically shrank him but had no apparent impact on his psychological state. He remained as busy and engaged as ever. It was obvious from his appearance that he was seriously unwell but his mind continued to be alert, his involvement with organizations like the Irish Georgian Society as active as before. 'He was amazingly stoic during his illness,' Catherine remembers. 'He was so unwell and in pain, but he didn't mutter a single moan.' A personal memory: I visited Desmond in hospital less than a month before his death and mentioned a newly published book on Irish houses I was reading. A week later I returned to see him again, and in the meantime he had obtained a copy of the book, read it and, although almost without voice, wanted to discuss it.

Desmond died on 15 September 2011. Ten days later, following Irish tradition, his body was laid out in an open oak casket in the hall at Glin Castle and the door left open so that visitors could call to pay their respects and say their farewells. The following afternoon, the coffin was placed on a century-old horse-drawn cart and, just as had been the case for Desmond's father and grandfather, slowly made its way down to the village beyond the castle gates, a long line of mourners led by Olda and his three daughters walking behind the cortège. They were met by uilleann piper Ronan Browne performing an Irish lament, 'The Chulainn'. Since Desmond had many years before donated the Church of Ireland premises to Glin Development Association, his funeral service was held in the Roman Catholic church, attended by a congregation numbering more than 800 including representatives of both the taoiseach and the president. Friends united in mourning had travelled from across Ireland, Britain and beyond to be present at an occasion that was both sorrowful and celebratory. Desmond's daughters Honor and Catherine read poems, as did Catherine's husband actor Dominic West, after which Eddie McParland gave the main address.

'Everything in his life centred on Glin and his life here,' Eddie declared of Desmond. 'From Glin radiated out those passionate commitments which embraced the whole of Ireland ... For this most cosmopolitan man, Ireland was the centre of the world and Glin was the centre of Ireland. He was the truly patriot Knight; An Ridire Tírgrách.' Afterwards the same horse and cart that had brought Desmond's coffin from the castle bore it to the nearby graveyard where, once more to the accompaniment of uilleann pipers, he was laid in the family plot.

'He never rested when he was alive,' Eddie had commented in the church, 'and I think he would hate the idea of heavenly rest. Instead, he will be forever energetically alive in our memory, and may he live forever in the memory of all who care for everything that's best about Ireland.

Long live the FitzGerald House of Glin. Shanid A Boo.'

Acknowledgments

MANY PEOPLE have assisted with the production of this book, and the author would like to thank the following for their kind support and recollections (and to apologize to anyone who has been inadvertently omitted): George Adams, Nelson Aldrich, Ken Bergin (University of Limerick), Donough Cahill and the staff of the Irish Georgian Society, Edward Clive, Professor Anne Crookshank, Bob Duff, James Fennell, Christopher Gibbs, Mark Girouard, David Griffin, the Hon. Desmond Guinness, Patrick Guinness, John Hamer, John and Eileen Harris, Peter Hebb, James and Mary Hobart, Min Hogg, Chris and Paul Johnston, Ciara Joyce (NUI Maynooth), William Laffan, Ronald Lightbown, Dr Edward McParland, Christopher Maule, Barry Mawhinney, David Mlinaric, Simon Mounsey, Helen O'Neill, Thomas Pakenham, James Peill, Florence Phillips, the Earl of Roden, John Rogers, Lord Rossmore, Christine Ryall, Alan Spence, George Stacpoole, John Stefanidis, Jay Stiefel, Sir Richard Temple, Nicholas White. Also Fiona Dunne, Marsha Swan, Kitty Lyddon and all the staff at The Lilliput Press.

A very special word of thanks to Elisabeth and H. Peter Haveles, Jr; Alan and Mary Hobard; Elizabeth Dater Jennings; The J.M. Kaplan Fund, Richard D. Kaplan and Edwina Sandys; Fred and Kay Krehbiel; Michael and Helen Roden.

And, of course, particular thanks to Olda FitzGerald and to Catherine, Nesta and Honor FitzGerald for generously agreeing to and assisting with the publication of this work, together with the hope that they feel it does justice to Desmond.

It will be clear that Desmond FitzGerald wrote and published extensively throughout his life. A full bibliography would have demanded a lot of additional pages here, but readers interested in his publications are recommended to see the Irish Georgian Society's journal *Irish Architectural and Decorative Studies Vol. X*, which has a full bibliography of Desmond up to the end of 2007, by which date the greater number of his works had appeared in print.

Photographs of the entrance hall at Glin today and of the library at Glin after the May 2009 sale are courtesy of James Fennell (www.jamesfennell.com). All other images courtesy of Glin Castle.

Index